WESTERN FRONT 1917–1918 THE COST OF VICTORY

An Australian working party, with gas-mask kits worn on the chest and legs gaitered with sandbags, negotiates a duck-board track through the shell-blasted, boggy landscape at Zonnebeke, scene of fierce fighting during the Third Ypres offensive in September 1917. The twisted barbed-wire entanglements mark the recent German front line captured by Australian troops.

Australia 1788-1988

AUSTRALIANS AT WAR

WESTERN FRONT 1917–1918 THE COST OF VICTORY

JOHN LAFFIN

TIME-LIFE BOOKS. AUSTRALIA
in association with JOHN FERGUSON. SYDNEY

Designed and produced by
John Ferguson Pty Ltd
100 Kippax Street
Surry Hills, NSW 2010

Series Editor: John Ferguson
Consulting Editor: George C. Daniels
Series Director: Lesley McKay
Editor: Tony Love
Picture Editor: Candace Campbell
Designer: Jane Tenney
Production Manager: Phillipa Denton
Production Assistant: Tracy O'Shaughnessy
Staff Writer / Picture Researcher: Julian Leatherdale
Assembly Artist: Josie Howlett

Time-Life Books, South Pacific Books Division
Managing Director: Bonita L. Boezeman
Production Manager: Ken G. Hiley

The Author: JOHN LAFFIN is one of the world's best known war historians. His background is military, as both his parents served in the first AIF — his mother as a nurse, and his father in the infantry. Dr Laffin and his wife Hazelle visit Australian battlefields all over the world and are, in fact, the only Australian battlefield archeologists. He has written more than 100 books, of which about half concern military history. One of his best known books is *Digger: The Legend of the Australian Soldier.* He has also written *Western Front 1916-1917, The Price of Honour,* another in this series.

First published in 1988 by
Time-Life Books (Australia) Pty Ltd
15 Blue Street
North Sydney, NSW 2060

© Time-Life Books (Australia) Pty Ltd 1988

This book is copyright. Apart from any fair dealing for the purposes of private study, research, criticism or review, as permitted under the Copyright Act, no part may be reproduced by any process without written permission. Inquiries should be addressed to the publisher.

National Library of Australia
cataloguing-in-publication data

Laffin, John, 1922-
    Western Front II

    Bibliography.
    Includes index.
    ISBN O 949118 20 6.
    1. World War, 1914-1918 — Australia.
    2. World War, 1914-1918 — Campaigns — Belgium.
    3. World War, 1914-1918 — Campaigns — France.
    I. Title. (Series: Australians at War; 8).

940.4'3

This publication has been partially funded by the Australian Bicentennial Authority as part of its program to help celebrate Australia's Bicentennial in 1988.

Printed in Hong Kong.

CONTENTS

Chapter	1	**Shouldering Arms for Ypres**	**8**
Picture Essay		Charity Begins at Home	18
	2	**The Battles Down Menin Road**	**26**
		On Menin Road	46
	3	**Germany's Devastating Offensive**	**54**
		Out of the Old Kit Bag	81
	4	**Turning the Tables**	**90**
		Heroes Without Guns	106
	5	**East of Amiens**	**114**
		Digger	132
	6	**The Climax and the Cost**	**142**

Bibliography	164
Picture Essay Quotes	164
Acknowledgments	165
Picture Credits	165
Index	166

Australian photographer Frank Hurley's famous composite photograph "Over the Top" combines two trench-line photos with superimposed shell bursts and

roaring aircraft to capture the fearful confusion of battle. Hurley argued: "It is impossible to secure full effects of this bloody war without composite pictures."

1
SHOULDERING ARMS FOR YPRES

All five AIF divisions were now battle-hardened, and with Allied forces consolidated on Messines Ridge, the stage was set for a massive eastwards offensive. But the 3rd Division AIF had to overcome Flanders' fields of mud and German opposition as fierce as ever.

In the middle of 1917 the overall situation of the First World War was critical for the Allies. The British had been victorious at Messines in June, mainly because of the dash and determination of the Australians and New Zealanders, but it was a relatively minor operation in the great movements of the war as a whole. Elsewhere, success was elusive.

In May the Italians, who had joined the Allies in 1915, attacked the Austrian Army in the Alps only to be thrown back with heavy losses. Mutinies were racking the French Army and its morale was in tatters. The United States had entered the war; fresh American troops would be arriving before long. And the tank had become a major offensive weapon. French Commander-in-Chief Marshal Henri Petain wanted to wait until the British and French had enough of the armoured behemoths before staging his next offensive.

For a short time, it seemed that Allied military fortunes were improving. The Russians launched a major attack on the Eastern Front mainly against the Austrian Army, while the British were in the last stages of preparation for

Australian war artist Will Dyson's sketch "Australian Tunnellers near Nieuport" shows the claustrophobic, dangerous world of tunnelling warfare.

the coming Ypres offensive. The eastern attack began on July 1, but within days it collapsed and the Russian Army became a rabble.

It was distressingly clear to the British government, and especially to its Prime Minister, David Lloyd George, that for the next four or five months the British Army in Flanders would be fighting alone. Even more alarming was the realisation that the Germans and Austrians, without pressure from the French, Italians and Russians, could heavily reinforce their front opposite the British in Flanders. Lloyd George opposed British offensives if there were to be no French offensives. Petain, however, urged the British to attack so that the French Army would have time to recover.

The ever aggressive British commander, Sir Douglas Haig, was only too anxious to oblige. Haig proposed to break through the strongest defences of the entire front, even if the British had to do it unaided. He argued for an all-out offensive, though Lloyd George and his Cabinet desired only a step-by-step victory in the Messines style. The step-by-step method used massed artillery to batter a limited depth of German defences, then sent in infantry to occupy the evacuated ground, and called forward the artillery to repeat the process. Haig did not agree with this policy and favoured the principles of the Somme offensive. This meant a combination of what he called "wearing down" and "breaking-through" tactics.

Haig's strategy terrified every member of the War Committee, consisting of Lloyd George, Lord Curzon, Lord Milner and the South African leader, Jan Smuts. They feared that the enormous task to which Haig was setting the British and Imperial armies might well prove to be a fatal mistake. But the War Committee could suggest no better alternative. Haig had his way, largely because Lloyd George believed that if the offensive was not successful after a week or two he could persuade Haig to stop.

Anticipating the British offensive, the Germans did not merely strengthen their defences, they attacked. The assault took place on July 10 at the extreme left of the Allied line, where units of General Sir Henry Rawlinson's Fourth Army clung to a small bridgehead in German-held territory across the Yser River.

At the time, the 2nd Australian Tunnelling Company was mining in the sand dunes just northeast of the Yser's outlet, where the Allied line met the Belgian coast. Using methods adapted from goldfield mining, the Australian miners made two deep dugouts and then tunnelled horizontally from them. They penetrated out into No-Man's-Land, heading for the enemy lines. About 50 of them were hard at work when the Germans attacked. A few Australians were killed in the fighting and some others struggled across the Yser River to safety but most of the miners were captured.

Rawlinson had intended to make an advance along the coast from the Yser bridgehead as a minor part of Haig's Ypres offensive. The German attack was a setback, but part of the bridgehead still lay in Rawlinson's hands and he was able to modify rather than change his plans. His subsidiary attack was not expected to have any effect on the war; it was merely intended to stretch the Germans' capacity to resist the main British offensive.

The Australian Imperial Force (AIF) was ready for it. With the end of the Battle of Messines all five divisions had been in battle. Even the men of the 3rd Division, the last to see action, now felt like veterans. For them, as for the men of the more experienced divisions, there was no exultation, no sense of glory; they had seen too many of their mates killed by bullets, shrapnel balls, shell shards and hand grenades. The survivors, having come through a great and fearful test, were proud of their performance. Militarily they had been efficient, and as men they had not broken under the stress of battle. Senior Australian officers were satisfied with the effectiveness of their units. The British Army and Corps commanders assessed the 3rd Division as an elite formation comparable with its fellow divisions.

The 3rd was paid compliments by all the leaders — from the Second Army Commander, General Sir Herbert Plumer, down to its own

Marshal Henri Petain, commander of the demoralised French Army receives a decoration from the British monarch, George V. Petain opposed British Commander Haig's planned Ypres offensive, but, with the King's backing, Haig went ahead.

divisional leader, the ambitious Major General John Monash, who had commanded a brigade at Gallipoli and whose competence had been noted since his arrival in the European theatre of war. To the men themselves, what counted most was their acceptance by the veterans of the other Australian divisions. It was particularly satisfying for the 3rd to be treated as equals by the 4th Division, in close support on the Messines front. The 4th, which had seen more action in 1917 than any other Australian division, no longer regarded the 3rd as new boys, babies and merely "men in uniform".

The 4th's veterans now greeted those of the 3rd with an affable, "Your mob seems to be doing all right," and with the familiar "G'day, Digger." The term was now universal in the AIF. The camaraderie meant that there was no longer a junior AIF division.

Confidence in Plumer's leadership was high among the Australians, who were part of his Second Army. His use of 19 great mines to blow the Germans off Messines Ridge before committing his infantry to battle stamped him as a thinking general. His stunning blow had eliminated the small bulging salient which the Germans had driven into the larger British salient south of Ypres.

It had not been intended to push deeply at Messines, nevertheless the line was advanced and straightened as the 3rd and 4th Divisions captured one wrecked and fortified farm after another. The Warneton Line, on the southern flank of the Ypres Salient, had been the Germans' third reserve line; now it was their front line.

Under fire, the 3rd Division's 11th Brigade, under Brigadier J.H. Cannan, dug a new system of defences for the main Australian front. It took them 18 dangerous and exhausting days and nights, and they suffered many casualties including, on July 6, Lieutenant Colonel F.J. Board of the 41st Battalion and his entire staff. On the same day, as the staff of the 4th Brigade HQ sat down to dinner, a 5.9-inch shell burst among them, killing two officers and wounding five, including brigade commander Brigadier General E.H. Brand.

Those 18 days were marked by outstanding co-operation between AIF infantry, engineers and pioneers. The engineers were the specialists in the building of defensive works. The pioneers, while able to fight as infantry, were the soldier-workers who prepared tracks and roads, often ahead of the infantry. Under the direction of two or three expert engineers or pioneers, scores of infantry working parties transformed the front line into a formidable defensive system. The old enemy front line became a traffic trench and from it a series of bays with fire steps and linking traverses were made in front. Cross-trenches were dug between the new front line and support line. The battalions used old German concrete dugouts as their headquarters.

Important visitors sometimes reached the Australian lines. One was the Premier of New South Wales, W.A. Holman. The commander of the 4th Division, Major General W. Holmes, escorted him on a tour of the Messines battlefield, and because he had a civilian to protect, Holmes did not take the shortest and

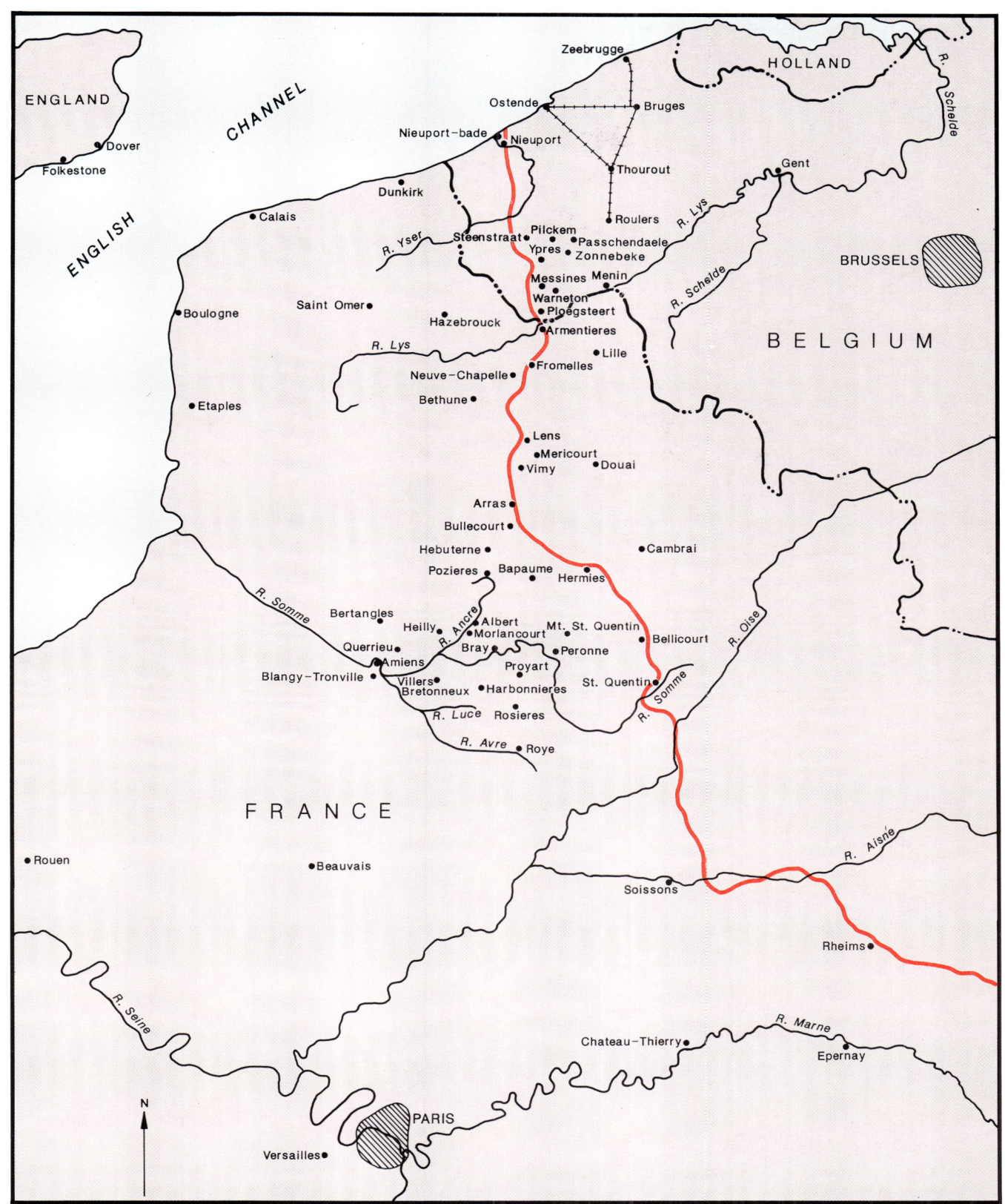

After two-and-a-half years of fighting, the Western Front's trench lines were still concentrated in the Lys River and Somme River and the French sector to the south. In June 1917 the Allied armies made great gains in their successful assault at Messines, the first in a series of offensives to rid the Ypres Salient of entrenched German forces. The next attack, to be fought on the last day of July, was called the Battle of Pilckem Ridge and proved a great success for the Australians involved.

Miners of the 2nd Australian Tunnelling Company rest near the entrance to their subterranean labyrinth in sand dunes at Nieuport on the Belgian coast. Most of the Company were captured in a surprise attack on July 10.

most dangerous route. Instead, he left his car and led his party on foot. At a normally safe spot a salvo of enemy shells landed almost on top of them, but only Holmes was hit. Wounded through chest and lung, he died of wounds an hour later. His death was a serious loss as Holmes's 4th Division was considered by many generals to be the best in the AIF. Major General E.W. Sinclair-Maclagan, who had ably commanded the 3rd Brigade for two years before being sent to supervise AIF training in England, was at once ordered to France to take Holmes's place.

With the British and Australian hold on Messines Ridge consolidated, the way was open for the more important offensive which Haig, now a Field Marshal, planned to deliver from Ypres, or "Wipers" as the troops called it. The official British title for the operation was "The Battles of Ypres 1917". Haig had three consecutive objectives. The first was to capture the Passchendaele to Gheluvelt ridge, though ridge was a misleading term for the arc of gently rising ground 10 kilometres east of Ypres. Possession of this higher ground would give security to Ypres, observation towards the east and a jumping-off point for an advance to the Belgian submarine port of Zeebrugge. The push would have several phases.

The second objective was the strategic railway which ran through Roulers and Thourout. The final objective, another 16 kilometres further on was a line from Courtrai to Zeebrugge. In the event, neither the second nor third objectives was achieved.

In all, 40 divisions, six of them French, were gathered in Flanders. Thirty-five of them, comprising three armies, would attack on a 24-kilometre front between Warneton and Steenstraat. On the right, or south, was Plumer's Second Army of 13 divisions spread over 10 kilometres of front. In the centre, where the main thrust was to take place, was General Sir Hubert Gough's Fifth Army of 16 divisions. On the north, or left, was General P. Anthoine's First French Army, with a front of only three kilometres. Another five divisions formed a separate force under General Rawlinson, who was to attack only when the Germans were being driven from the Passchendaele Ridge. The Australian divisions, when and how needed, came under Fifth Army command.

The first phase of the attack was the Battle of Pilckem Ridge. Again, it was merely higher ground rather than a ridge. North east of Ypres, its possession was necessary before another phase could become operational; its timetable was July 31 to August 2.

Haig's plan of attack depended on a tremendous British bombardment to obliterate German artillery and machine-gun emplacements. On the British Fifth Army's front there was an artillery piece to every five-and-a-half metres — an incredible 3,091 guns in all. The two divisions of French troops, grudgingly given to Haig for use on his left flank, had 1,040 guns, one to every two metres on a 2,400-metre front. The massively heavy bombardment began on July 15, and in a 10-day period sent four-and-a-half tonnes of explosive metal crashing onto each metre of enemy front.

Despite the awful pounding, the Germans on the higher ground were constantly able to observe every British movement on the flat ground around Ypres. Even when guns were moved by night it was easy for skilled German observers to spot them next day, sometimes with the help of their fliers, and bring their own artillery to bear.

The Australian gunners suffered more severely from German shelling during the pre-offensive bombardment at Ypres than in any other action. Casualties were so heavy that AIF headquarters staff officers knew they would have to find artillery reinforcements on a similar scale to those of infantry units. The 4th Division's artillery alone lost four officers and 117 men from a complement of 600 in the three weeks before the infantry battle. Even so, the Australian effort did not slacken. Immediately before the attack, the thousands of guns on the battlefield commenced a continuous 12-hour shelling, with great strain on the men and their weapons. The gunners said that when they ceased fire the guns were so hot that water could be boiled on them — it was not far from the literal truth.

The great offensive began at 3.50 am on July 31. The only Australian division heavily engaged at that moment was the 3rd, which had been rested after its great effort at Messines. The 4th Division, now settled in under Major General Sinclair-Maclagan, was in close support. The role of the 3rd, from its positions at Messines on the right of the Allied line, was to feint at the German-held city of Lille. The hope was that the German High Command would believe that this was the axis of the main assault, but the Germans were not deceived, and from the beginning they knew that Haig's true objective was the ridge at Passchendaele, 32 kilometres north of Lille.

The feint, vigorously carried out by the 42nd and 43rd Battalions, provided several splendid examples of how the AIF chain of command functioned in the heat of battle. At the centre of the attack, German bomb throwers checked a company of the 43rd Battalion. The commander, Lieutenant F.G. Tucker, ran forward and his men followed. When Tucker fell wounded, Lieutenant K. Dunstan took his place, only to be himself wounded. Instantly, Sergeant J. Barraclough assumed command and captured the next German post. Wounded, he still continued to direct operations until the situation was secure.

In the platoon attacking a nearby enemy position, the subaltern commander and both sergeants were wounded, but Corporal S.J. McLaughlin rallied the men and led them on to capture the objective. Away to the right, two platoons attacked strongly held positions in the ruins of a windmill. When Lieutenant W.G. Harrington and all officers and sergeants were wounded, Corporal E.E.V. Roberts shouted that he was now giving the orders. Under his vigorous leadership the mill was captured. Roberts was awarded the Distinguished Conduct Medal.

Another brand of Australian initiative was also demonstrated in the fight. Lieutenant A.S. Varley of the AIF's 9th Light Trench Mortar

Packhorses, laden with 18-pounder shells, stumble through thick mud on Pilckem Ridge on August 1, 1917. On first seeing the mud, Haig's chief-of staff later cried, "Good God, did we really send men to fight in that?"

A compassionate Tommy gives a light to a German soldier who lies wounded in No-Man's-Land, one of the 50 prisoners taken in the Battle of Pilckem Ridge on July 31, 1917.

Battery had invented a new kind of smoke bomb for use with Stokes mortars. Varley's bombs, which emitted slow, heavy and lingering smoke, unlike the usual smoke which quickly dissipated, undoubtedly saved the lives of many Australians as they advanced under its cover.

At mid-morning of the first day, the Germans launched a fierce counter-attack against the Australians and managed to recapture a key position, the ruins of a windmill known as Post VII. The 43rd Battalion's Commanding Officer, Lieutenant Colonel C.P. Butler, ordered his reserve company to get the position back, but all its platoons were already committed. Hurrying about the posts and trenches, Sergeant G.P. Rayner collected 40 men, but his attack was stopped by heavy fire. Locating a platoon of the 41st Battalion, Rayner asked its commander, Lieutenant P.W. Harrison, a Gallipoli veteran of great ability, to pin down the Germans with fire from the front. Then, in a brilliant little manoeuvre, Rayner led his 40 men around the German flank and seized the post. Few Germans escaped.

From the Australian point of view, the first day of the Battle of Ypres was a complete success. The cost had been 500 casualties to the 11th Brigade, yet they had retained all the captured positions. Heavy rain then flooded them but the Australians, though miserably wet, held on.

Field Marshal Haig saw the results of the first day's fighting in the main offensive as "most satisfactory", but this was not actually so. While parts of General Gough's Fifth Army had reached the German second line, on his southern or right flank, his troops had captured only the first line. In another way, the situation was highly unsatisfactory. The tremendous Allied bombardment and the consequent German counter-fire had torn the countryside to shreds, destroying the intricate drainage system of the flat land. At 4 pm on July 31, heavy rain began to fall — and it did not stop. Every shell hole and mine crater filled with water and virtually every ditch and stream had been dammed by shell-torn earth. Within a few hours, the entire battlefield was a morass.

With great effort, men could walk, but guns, lorries and carts were hopelessly bogged. Supplies could not reach the infantry and nobody knew for sure where some units were because communications were badly disrupted. Many British shells failed to explode in the soft mud, which muffled the explosions of those that did burst. And the rain persisted for day after day into August. Flanders' fields turned into a foul mire of mud, and any action there would now result in appalling casualties. Although the AIF 1st, 2nd and 5th Divisions had been out of the line, while away from the action, they had been trained in a new method of attacking. This began with each unit advancing swiftly to evade the inevitable barrage which the Germans put down at the first sign of an attack. The advancing infantry would then be safely behind the falling German shells. The battalions would then quickly sort themselves into prearranged waves and the leading one would advance closely behind its own creeping artillery barrage. The barrage was designed to move forward very slowly, sometimes covering only 100 metres in eight minutes, compared with two minutes in the Somme. This gave the infantry time to capture any stubbornly held blockhouses. According to the new plan of attack, there would be several pauses in the advance, perhaps an hour or more, to permit all units making the advance to draw level.

Each of a battalion's 16 platoons now had rifle grenadiers and Lewis gunners to support the riflemen and bombers in attacks on blockhouses. It became the practice for the rest of the line to move forward and not to wait for the capture of a blockhouse, generally a protracted and bloody business. The delayed platoon would catch up as soon as it could. When, at the end of July, the Diggers of the 1st, 2nd and 5th Divisions were moved north into rear areas of Flanders, they were fit and rested and as highly trained as any units on the Western Front.

At this period the Australian artillery, detached from its own divisions, was still heavily and dangerously engaged. Infantry

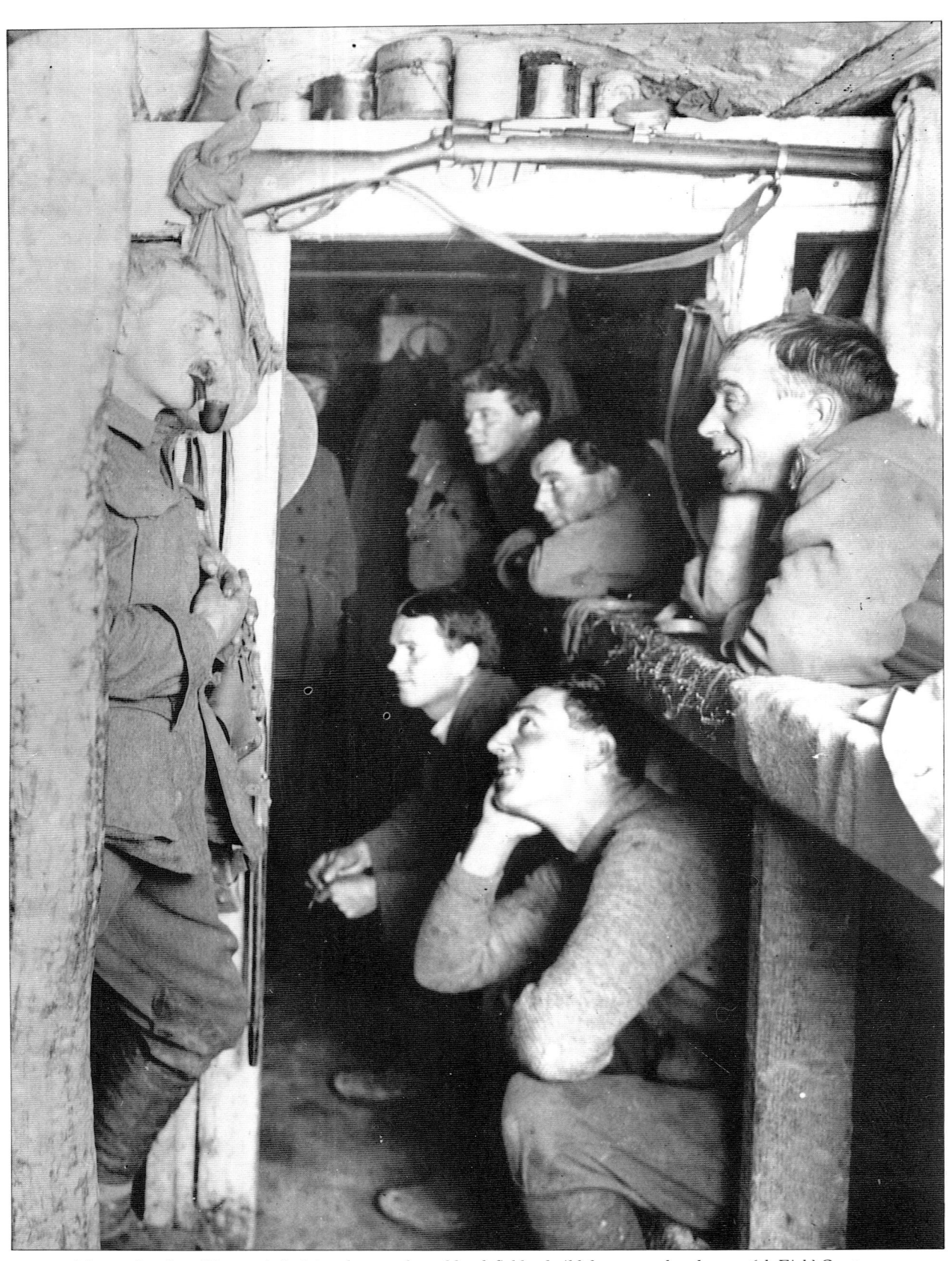

After weeks of gruelling work draining the waterlogged battlefield to build dugouts and pathways, 6th Field Company engineers relax in their cosy billet in the dry and shellproof vaults of Ypres' historic ramparts.

units were frequently relieved but the gunners had to stay on, supporting one division after another. The gunners themselves said that the bravest men were the artillery drivers, who day and night took their horse-drawn wagons through enemy barrages to get ammunition to the guns. Major R.G. Manton, commanding the 15th Battery, told a war correspondent, "Wagon-driving was looked on almost as a cold-footed job before, one which did not take a man into action. But like all those Australians who were supposed to be in fairly safe jobs, the drivers take a pride in showing what they can do when they come into the thick of battle."

The 1st, 2nd and 5th Divisions were camped and billeted in the area around Hazebrouck, in French Flanders. In this town was the HQ of General Sir William Birdwood, who still held overall command of the five Australian and the one New Zealand divisions. The 1st Division HQ was also in Hazebrouck and in the nearby hill town of Cassel were British Second Army HQ and Haig's advanced HQ. The AIF men arrived in the region with remarkable reputations for sobriety and discipline, but within days they were accused of being riotous in Cassel. It was true that men of two units demonstrated noisily, but they believed they had a right to do so. A sergeant of the British military police had arrested an Australian for being drunk. His mates objected, saying that he was stone cold sober, and called up as reinforcements every Australian within earshot. The tension subsided with the arrival of the Australian Assistant Provost Marshal, Major W. Smith. Having restored order, Major Smith asked the British sergeant why he believed the Australian soldier was drunk.

"He had to be, sir," the sergeant said. "Otherwise he wouldn't have come up to a provost sergeant on duty and asked for the address of the nearest brothel."

Major Smith explained that to an Australian soldier the approach seemed logical. A provost sergeant, in the line of duty, would naturally know the location of all brothels. He then explained to the crowd of Australians that there had been a misunderstanding, the arrested soldier was released and the so-called riot ended. Nevertheless, Cassel was placed out of bounds to the AIF. Such ludicrous incidents were often the basis of the Australians' undeserved reputation for wild behaviour.

Field Marshal Haig reviewed the 2nd and 5th Divisions on parade on August 29 and commented to Major General Brudenell White, the AIF's chief staff officer, that they could not have marched better had they endured years of peacetime training. White, who had been largely responsible for winning the Australians their long rest, already knew this.

The 3rd Division came out of the line after the success of its feint attack, but the much-used 4th Division, depleted and tired, was not withdrawn to rest until mid-August. C.E.W. Bean, the ever-present official war correspondent, was with the Diggers in Flanders in August and September 1917. He noticed that, at least in the well rested and reinforced 1st, 2nd and 5th Divisions, a "marked eagerness" came over the men as action became imminent.

"Each man had faced up to whatever private problems this battle had in store for him," Bean said. " There flew around the messes grim jokes as to whom should inherit his friend's boots or binoculars, and, despite old dreads and horrid memories, men were obviously keen to put into use the drill they had been practising and confident that they could outplay the enemy. The excitement of the great game, which must be won, mingled with their other feelings."

Three Diggers visit ladies of the Australian Comforts Fund who are sewing and packaging kangaroo skin vests and woollen shirts for the boys abroad.

EVERY PENNY COUNTS

Rarely did a day pass during the First World War when the average Australian was not exhorted either personally or by poster or leaflet to make a financial contribution to the war effort. Apart from the staggering £274 million raised by seven government war loan campaigns, a vast array of privately run patriotic funds and charities bombarded the public with appeals to dig deep into their pockets.

The Australian branch of the British Red Cross Society, and the nationwide Australian Comforts Fund grew into huge fund-raising bureaucracies staffed by an unpaid army of women administrators and workers. At the regional and local level countless women's charity groups sprung up in keen rivalry to help the cause. These private bodies filled an important gap by providing the troops with warm clothing and comforts packages, by supervising the care and rehabilitation of returned soldiers and by raising relief funds for civilian wartime victims in Allied Europe.

Over £13 million was raised during the war years by these funds from bazaars, street fairs and processions, costume balls, garden parties, dances and public meetings. When the streets weren't filled with parades, one could still be accosted by cake sellers, button sellers and door-to-door collectors. The Red Cross even commissioned commercial films to raise funds through box office profits.

The war-loan subscribers and charity donors came predominantly from the middle and upper classes for they had the capacity to "give" generously. Working class families on the other hand, were often unfairly accused of disloyalty for failing to do their share for the home-front war effort, particularly when the community was divided over the conscription issue and union strikes. They had borne the brunt of war casualties and were understandably resentful.

As the public purse was squeezed for more funds the Australian people learned that running a war was indeed a costly business.

A starched white column of proud Volunteer Detachment Nurses marches between the tramlines of a Melbourne street on Red Cross Day, May 24, 1918. The Red Cross-recruited VADs were the home-front nursing corps.

Two volunteer workers cut strips of metal binding for boxes in the Red Cross packing department, the converted ballroom of Government House, Melbourne.

"Last night I went to a Red Cross bazaar." "Sorry, old man, I'm broke too." A Bulletin cartoon lampoons charitable middle-class "self-sacrifice".

An impressive exhibit of Christmas cakes awaiting shipment demonstrates the grand scale of Red Cross operations and the Society's flair for self-promotion. A newspaper from each state branch updated record-breaking work statistics.

Above: Costumed allegorically as the United Kingdom, six "loyalists" try to conquer stage fright in a patriotic fund-raising tableau on ice in Melbourne, 1915. Below: Wearing the emblem of the YMCA, volunteers sell refreshments during the "Red Triangle Day" street campaign held in Martin Place, Sydney, in June 1917 which raised over £100,000.

Left: Adapted from a French war-loan poster, a postcard urges greater fund-raising efforts for victory. Similar national days were organised for Belgium. Above: A stern war-bond poster on an automobile, exploits the pathos of Belgium's torment.

In a France's Day motorcar procession through Sydney, a French child in military costume stands to sing "The Marseillaise". A tiny "Digger" sits loyally at his side while children in national dress collect from the crowd.

Advertising the subscription figures for government war bonds, large mock tanks in Melbourne graphically express how every penny invested

in war loans pays for the military effort abroad. Some war loans posters even illustrated the point with an enemy soldier crushed by a gigantic shilling.

2
THE BATTLES DOWN MENIN ROAD

The Allied thrust continued towards Passchendaele. After a series of ridges fell to the AIF in desperate fighting, the worn-out Anzac divisions spearheaded a major assault at Broodseinde. But victory there was costly, and Australian forces now faced a chronic manpower crisis.

In wintry rain, a Digger carries kindling for a billet fire in Dyson's "Gathering Fuel. Delville Wood, 1917".

On the very day, August 29, 1917, that Haig inspected the AIF 2nd and 5th Divisions, he, General Plumer and the corps commanders knew that the task of capturing the key position on Passchendaele Ridge would be given to I Anzac Corps. It had also been decided that II Anzac Corps would enter the battle first to relieve and then support I Anzac.

General Birdwood, commanding I Anzac, was anxious for Australian divisions to operate in pairs. One of his divisional commanders, Major General H.B. Walker of the 1st Division, had told him that the mere fact of serving beside other Australian divisions increased the efficiency of his own division by 30 per cent. Birdwood suggested that the 4th Division, then part of II Anzac Corps, should be returned to his own Corps, I Anzac. As well, II Anzac, which consisted of the New Zealand Divisions and the 3rd AIF Division, would be reinforced with two British divisions. At that time, there seemed to be no way in which all five AIF divisions could be kept together. As the 4th Division came out of the line at Messines it found itself transferred to I Anzac and the men greeted the news with delight. The 3rd Division was not so ecstatic. It had always been happy alongside the New Zealanders, but the presence of two British divisions in the same corps was unsettling.

Neither Birdwood nor White wanted to make too much of the AIF's lack of confidence in British troops, but it was a strong feeling nonetheless. In fact, many British divisions were well led, hard-fighting formations and not inferior to the Australian divisions. But they operated to a different internal system which was more rigid than in Australian units. Unit commanders did not have the freedom of decision of their Australian counterparts and thus could not seize opportunities as they arose on the battlefield. The Diggers constantly feared that their flanks might be exposed by their British comrades not keeping up with the Australians' pace.

Meanwhile, the German High Command had introduced a new type of defence to meet the anticipated British assault on the heights of the Ypres Salient. At the front, defined trench lines did not exist as they did elsewhere on the Western Front. The Germans held their forward line only by scattered infantry posts. In a wide band behind them were medium machine-guns arranged in such a fashion that each post, generally in a pillbox or blockhouse, was covered by at least two others. Behind these defences lay heavily manned support trenches, reserve trenches and even more machine-guns. The Germans proposed to allow the British to penetrate the forward positions and then wipe them out in rapid counter-attacks made by special assault battalions.

Plumer's Second Army, first with the I Anzac and British X Corps as its spearhead, and then II Anzac, was to attack on September 20 in the "Battle of the Menin Road". This road was the main west-east route, though the road itself was now untraceable in the mud, craters and shell holes. To gain control of this axis it was first necessary to capture "ridges", one of which was Veldhoek Ridge and the other Anzac Spur, where there was a dominating blockhouse overlooking Menin Road. Haig made his expectations of the two Anzac corps known to Brigadier General R.A. Carruthers, the Deputy Adjutant and Quarter Master General of I Anzac Corps, on August 29. "If the Anzac corps do their job the Germans will have to leave the Belgian coast and if you can keep up your efforts throughout September we shall have the Germans beaten," he said.

His general instruction, once again, was to "wear down" the enemy. In tactical terms, corps commanders were able to interpret this as they wished. For the Anzac formations, especially I Anzac, the tactical plan was again the responsibility of Major General Brudenell White, as Chief of Staff. White decided, and Birdwood concurred, that the men must not be pushed to exhaustion and that organisation must be maintained. In his view, an advance of close to 1,500 metres in a day was adequate and only in several stages. In this way the troops would remain fit and control would not be lost.

All attacks, White ordered, were to have a wide front. And no attack was to be allowed to degenerate into costly local operations. In this, White was echoing his superior, Plumer, who opposed small attacks to straighten the uneven front, especially after General Gough, commander of Fifth Army, was defeated in three attempts to straighten his lines, on September 6 and 7, and September 10. Gough had suffered 3,000 casualties in the process.

White's plan, which was approved by Plumer, was to seize heights, craters and German blockhouses and to build defences around them to resist the inevitable counter-attacks. Officers of the Anzac corps were told that on occasions when some position was taken, their men must dig in. In White's plan, the final stage of the advance to Veldhoek Ridge and Anzac Spur was to be short and steady because by then the men would be battle-weary.

With meticulous care, White evolved an artillery-fire plan. He wanted five successive lines of shells exploding all over the German positions to a depth of 900 metres. To achieve this he was given 1,295 guns. His 18-pounders would shell the first German positions;

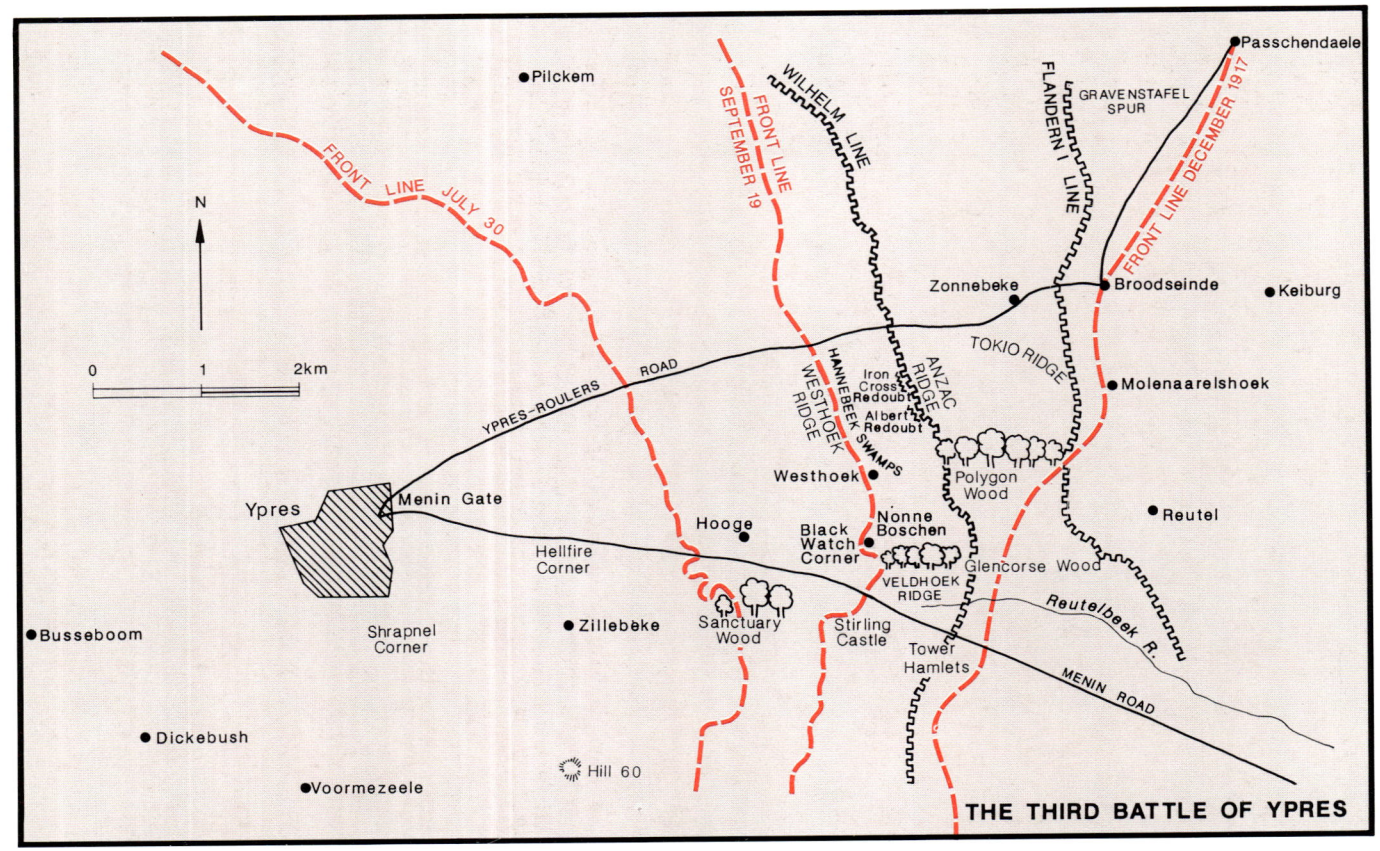

In order to force back the Germans from Ypres and to take Passchendaele, the Allies had to capture a series of fortified ridges. Eight assaults followed, the first three greatly influenced by AIF soldiers, who took the high ground north of Menin Road, then Polygon Wood, and finally Broodseinde.

18-pounders and the high-trajectory 4.5-inch howitzers their second line, 183 metres behind. At successive intervals of 183 metres on three more fire lines, the battering would be taken up by 6-inch, 8-inch and 9.2-inch howitzers. Throughout the storm of gunfire, massed machine-guns would rake the German positions to prevent even the most determined German infantry from moving through the shell-fire. For various eventualities, White used what he termed roaming, fixed, and emergency barrages. The roaming barrages, being deliberately random, were to perplex and surprise the enemy. The fixed fire went on pounding particular targets so that the Germans could not repair and return to them, while an emergency barrage would be available for any senior infantry commander who called for it. The combination was successful.

White realised that if I Anzac was to attack successfully it could not afford to use large numbers of troops to defend its right flank. Yet this would be exposed because the neighbouring British X Corps was not to go as far forward in the attack; its commander was therefore ordered to use an entire division to protect the Australians' flank.

White's attention to detail in planning was exemplary and senior AIF officers saw to it that all ranks understood the operation. Large models of the battlefield were laid out in fields and studied by thousands of troops. Standard military message forms were given another dimension: on the back of the forms White had printed maps of the ground to be fought over, together with useful notes about the condition of tracks. When an officer or NCO sent a message to his headquarters he could refer it to positions he marked on the map. It was an excellent idea and White was the first to use it.

Under camouflage nets in Ypres, Australian gunners prepare to fire their 9.5-inch howitzer. The dawn barrage on September 20, 1917 broke, in war historian C.E.W. Bean's words, "With the suddenness of a great orchestra."

On September 16 the tense but determined attack troops began to enter the forward zone and were bivouacked in all available shelter, including a captured German tunnel under Menin Road. Others sheltered behind the battered but still stout ramparts of the ruined town of Ypres. The fight the Australians were going into was called the "Battle of the Menin Road", but more accurately it was a battle to control Menin Road ridge, the high ground which the road crossed on the way to Menin itself. Menin Road was a famous name in the Ypres Salient, if only because so many soldiers left the ruins of Ypres through this gate in the city walls on their way to battle, and so many did not come back. The road travelled due east to the front line, and was the artery of the battlefield. Along it in both directions moved columns of men, wagons, ambulances and guns.

Security was essential and Birdwood ordered his officers to take every precaution against allowing the Australian presence to become known before the attack. If the German High Command was to find out that the much-feared Australian troops were mounting an attack, it would heavily reinforce the threatened front.

Soon after dark on the eve of battle, signals, engineer and pioneer officers put up signposts for each unit and laid tapes for direction-finding and for the start line. The front tapes were less than 150 metres distant from the nearest German positions. Everything that could be done to make the offensive a success had been done. British and Australian artillery had been pounding the German lines for five days. From the AIF commanders' point of view only one decision was wrong. They had wanted to attack at 5.10 am, the time at which a man would be just visible at 150 metres. General Plumer, however, decided on 5.40 am.

Shortly before the start time an officer of the 2nd Division's 7th Machine-Gun Company was misdirected and ran into a German patrol. He desperately tried to tear to pieces an operations order he was carrying, but the Germans overpowered him. Thus warned, the German

Perched on a fallen beam, a soldier contemplates the dormant ruins of St. Martin's Cathedral in Ypres. Caught in the ebb and flow of battle since 1914, "Wipers" was heavily bombarded by German artillery.

command bombarded the sector shown on the map at 5.35 am. Some casualties occurred but the start was not delayed and at 5.40 am on the fine, dry morning of September 20 no fewer than 11 divisions of the Second and Fifth Armies struck the Germans on a 13-kilometre front. The AIF 1st and 2nd Divisions, with a combined front of 1,800 metres, and a Scottish division, were at the centre of the assault force along Westhoek Ridge and facing Glencorse Wood. This was the first occasion in the war on which two Australian divisions attacked side by side and the men were excited about it. AIF officers had difficulty in explaining this elation to British and other Allied officers. It was a matter of extended mateship, of knowing that other battalions of Australians were in support and relying implicitly on them.

As General White had planned, all waves of the Australian infantry advanced in a single line just behind the heavy protective barrage of bursting shells. With one gun to every four-and-a-half-metres, the rolling barrage churned up curtains of dust, and to C.E.W. Bean, who was yet again present to record the AIF's operations, it looked for all the world like an Outback dust storm blowing up. Following the remorseless battering ram of shells, the Australians overcame enemy infantry opposition and advanced steadily for almost a kilometre to their first objective, known as the Red Line. It ran along a sunken road, the north edge of Glencorse Wood to Hannebeek Swamp and bogs in the Nonne Boschen Copse. The first phase had gone well. After an hour's pause, while each unit was reorganised and resupplied by the carrying parties which followed them, they followed their artillery's barrage another 500 metres to the second objective, the Blue Line. This was fixed from Iron Cross Redoubt in the north to Albert Redoubt, Verbeck Farm and part of Polygon Wood in the south which they

The day before The Battle of Menin Road, 1st and 2nd Division troops gather near the Ypres moat, outside their billets in the sturdy ramparts which had withstood sieges since their construction in Napoleonic times.

also captured with spirited efficiency. It reflected their rehearsals.

Now they had a two-hour wait until they attacked the Germans' Wilhelm Line, which was roughly parallel to and 200 metres beyond the Blue Line. Lieutenant Colonel Wilder-Neligan, the brilliant, dashing and unorthodox commander of the 10th Battalion, had copies of the London *Daily Mirror* and the *Daily Mail* distributed among his two storm companies, as he called them. British officers passing through, German prisoners being shepherded back to the rear, and even other Australians were astonished to see Wilder-Neligan's men lying back in shell-holes as they ate their sandwiches, smoked captured German cigars and read their newspapers. They seemed oblivious to the surrounding roar of battle as they waited for their next orders.

Inevitably, German counter-shelling caused casualties. A company commander of the 8th Battalion, Captain D.G. Evans, was badly wounded but he refused to let the stretcher-bearers delay the unit's approach by picking him up. They returned for him later but he died of his wounds.

Where the Australians were held up, decisive action at junior level kept the momentum going. This was nowhere better shown than in the mud and debris of Glencorse Wood, where part of the 6th Battalion was stalled by a machine-gun in a pillbox. Second Lieutenant Fred Birks, together with Corporal W. Johnston, rushed it. Johnston was wounded by a bomb, but Birks killed the remainder of the enemy and captured the gun. Soon after this, he organised a small party and attacked another strong point occupied by about 25 Germans. Some of the enemy were killed and an officer and 15 men were captured. Like a man inspired, Birks reorganised a large number of Australians whose units had become entangled during the attack and consolidated

Lieutenant Fred Birks from Melbourne, was awarded a posthumous Victoria Cross for his gallant fighting on September 20, 1917.

the sector he had captured. A shell burst in a post of his company, burying several men. Birks, ignoring the explosions all round him, was desperately digging them out when another shell-burst killed him. His supreme gallantry and leadership in these three separate incidents did not go unrecognised; posthumously, he was honoured with the VC.

After the heat of localised fighting, the Australians detested what they regarded as treachery and showed no mercy to Germans guilty of it. Perhaps the most flagrant case occurred at the site of a massive blockhouse, codenamed Anzac in Australian plans. It should have been neutralised by the artillery barrage, but its machine-guns were still firing. Captain F.L. Moore's company of the 5th Battalion was losing men and the machine-guns posed even more of a threat to the next wave, because the men would expect to find them out of action.

Moore sent Company Sergeant Major H. Collins and 20 men to work around the blockhouse and attack from the rear.

The garrison made signals of surrender and Captain Moore ran forward. A German had dropped his light machine-gun and raised his hands. When he saw a single Australian officer coming towards him he grabbed up his gun, fired a burst into Moore and put up his hands again. Captain Moore's Victorian soldiers respected and loved him, and they at once killed the German and a number of his comrades. Only vigorous intervention by other AIF officers prevented them from slaughtering the entire garrison. Captain Moore died from his wounds that day and many men of the 5th Battalion swore they would never take another German prisoner.

Another grim incident took place when men of the 2nd Brigade surrounded a two-storey blockhouse and fired at upper loopholes from where shots were coming. One Australian was killed, but a few minutes later the enemy in the lower part of the small fortress surrendered. The Australians characteristically relaxed and some, with rifle butts between their feet, lit cigarettes. Then a shot was fired from an upper-storey loophole, killing an Australian. In wild anger at this breach of combat ethics, the Australians ran their bayonets through the prisoners. One man did not have his bayonet fixed to his rifle, but he quickly attached it and bayoneted a prisoner pleading for mercy.

The fighting on September 20 was a victory for the entire British force involved and especially so for the 1st and 2nd Divisions in their Battle of the Menin Road. By noon that hot day they had taken all their objectives and were at the western end of Polygon Wood. White's orders stressed that no troops were to go further than this, but adventurous individuals and small groups of Diggers crept forward in search of more prisoners and souvenirs. Many officers had by now given up trying to prevent this practice of "prospecting", which the soldiers of the other Allied armies regarded as lunacy, because of the risks.

Prime Minister William Hughes woos the crowd with impassioned rhetoric at a pro-conscription rally in Martin Place, Sydney, during the 1917 referendum campaign. He also addressed patriotic "women only" rallies to capture the female vote.

BLOOD BALLOT

The Great War generated a huge demand on Australia's resources. The regular monthly reinforcement quota of 11,790 officers and men was not enough, the Army Council decided on August 24, 1916, and it requested an immediate special draft of 20,000 infantry followed by 16,500 for each of the next three months.

Australia's volunteer system could not supply that number of men. It was the only country at war without conscription. The government of Prime Minister W.M. Hughes therefore asked the Australian people, through a referendum, to decide the question, "Should conscription be brought in for military service overseas?"

Probably no issue in Australian political history had so divided the country as did "the Blood Vote". Both sides had valid arguments, which they expressed emotionally and debated bitterly. The "Yes" lobby believed that their courageous and patriotic friends were bearing the brunt of the sacrifice. The "No" campaigners alleged that those who wanted conscription were largely people who would not have to go to the war anyway, being too old or unfit or otherwise exempt; they were callously breaking up families, the "No" lobby said, without themselves making any sacrifice.

In France, Belgium and Britain the troops voted by secret ballot, with 72,399 for conscription and 58,894 against. Most of those men actually at the front voted "No". Some did so because, they said, they would not bring their worst enemies into the hell of the Western Front. Other fighting men, including nearly all the officers and most of the NCOs, believed that proud volunteers should not have to mix with unwilling conscripts, and that the AIF's morale would suffer. "If they have to be forced to come, they won't be much use over here," was a common sentiment.

The national poll on October 28, 1916, produced 1,087,557 for conscription and 1,160,033 against, a majority against of 72,476.

The following year, after further heavy casualties and with the flow of volunteer reinforcements drying up, the government announced a second national referendum. Trade union officials opposed some recruiting methods and they were specially angry about an appeal asking every man whether he was prepared to enlist and if not, why not. Returned soldiers tarred and feathered an official of the Clerks Union who led the opposition to this inquiry.

On December 20, 1917, Australia again went to the polls: 1,015,159 voted for conscription and 1,181,747 opposed it, a majority against of 166,588. Among the armed forces the vote in favour was 103,789 with 93,910 against, but as in the earlier referendum the majority of front-line troops rejected conscription.

The acrimonious and emotional campaigns fought over the conscription issue did not help voluntary enlistment; recruiting fell to 1,518 in March 1918. During that year the AIF on the Western Front suffered a manpower shortage so serious that some officials believed that it could not continue to function effectively. Heavy casualties were directly responsible but, in addition, large numbers of soldiers were reaching the end of their endurance and were evacuated as unfit. Many of those who remained did so only through stubborn pride and mateship.

From May 1918, no AIF unit was at full strength and all became progressively weaker in numbers. The AIF began feeding upon itself, breaking up some units to strengthen others, and drawing reinforcements from training camps and depots. Some men coming out of hospital after treatment for wounds and illnesses were not given time to convalesce, and were sent straight back to their units. And few of the veterans at the training camps could be spared for the front. They were essential in turning Australian reinforcements into battle-ready soldiers. Even so, the veteran trainers often did not take kindly to the reinforcements. "You took long enough to get here," was a common welcome to newcomers to the Western Front.

Keep Australia White
Mr. Heitmann, Nationalist Member for Kalgoorlie, and a son of a German, speaking at Wedderburn during the Grampians by-election, stated
"Send every man out of Australia, even if they had to import black, brown or brindle labor to do their work."
CONSCRIPTION
FREEDOM
Vote No.

NO
LOYALTY
YES
BY VOTING "YES" AUSTRALIA WILL RUB OUT THIS BLOT

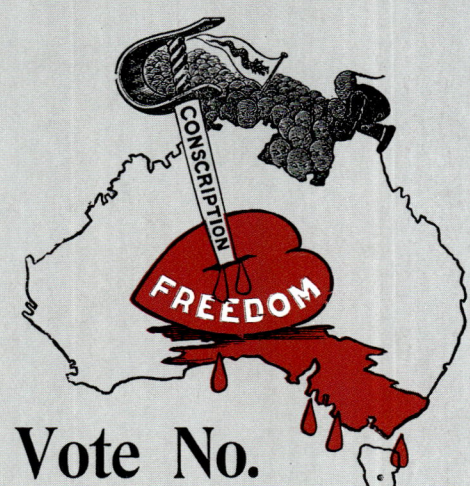

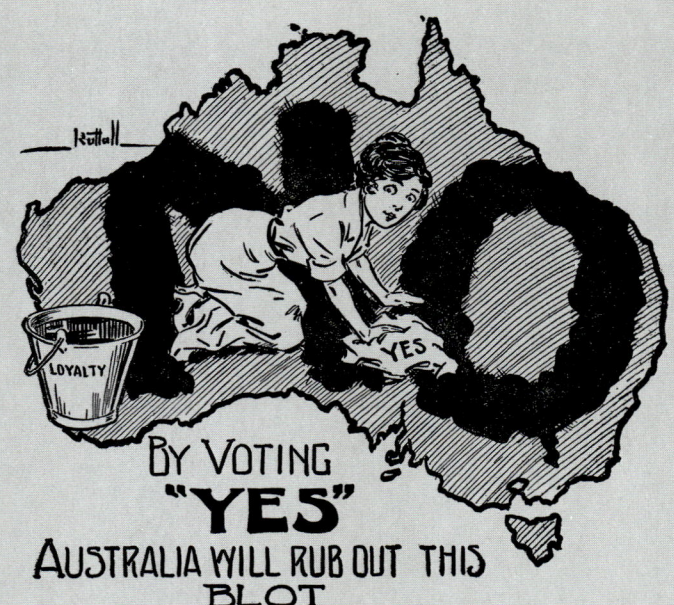

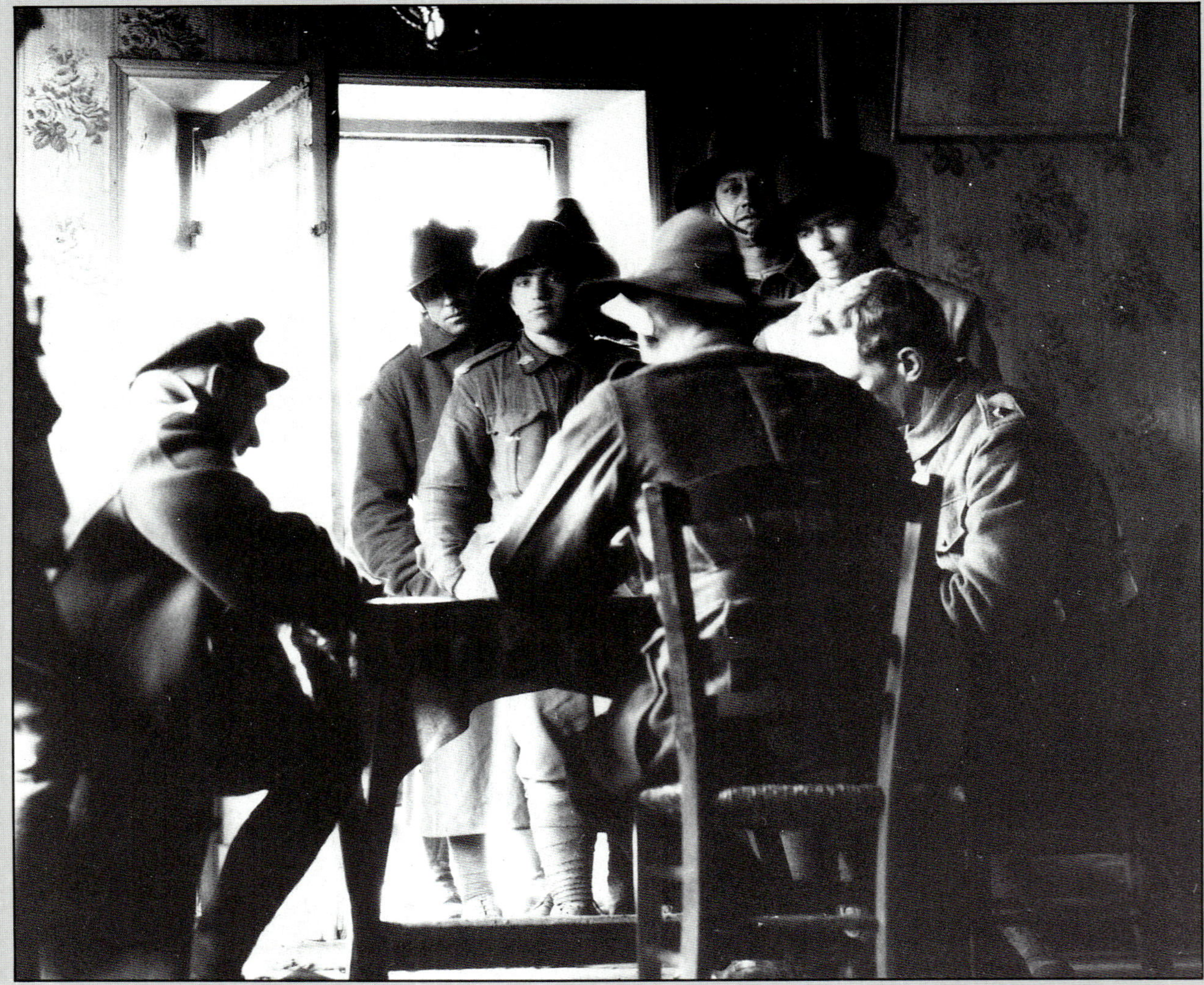

Top left: A 1916 "No" poster propagates rumours that conscripted men would lose their jobs to imported coloured labour and, equally unthinkable, to women. Top right: A 1917 "Yes" pamphlet calls on female patriotism to amend Australia's ties with Britain. Above: Troops in France cast their vote by secret ballot on December 8, 1917.

The most notorious pamphlet of the bitter "propaganda war" before both referenda, "The Blood Vote" poem was produced by the "No" lobby in 1916. The "Yes" campaign answered with "A Mother's Lament", another ballad of guilt.

Amid the debris of their weapons, three German soldiers cut down by the British barrage of September 20, 1917, lie huddled together in death. The maddening roar of the shell-fire drove them from their pillbox near Zonnebeke.

The British-Australian barrage had been in progress for eight hours and it now ceased. When the German counter-attacks began two hours later the guns opened again. None of the enemy attacks reached the Australian infantry. The 1st Division suffered 2,754 casualties in the battle and the 2nd received 2,259; they were severe losses but fewer proportionately than the British divisions. Overall, the British toll was between 20,000 and 25,000 men and German casualties were roughly the same, more than half being incurred on the Australian front. In addition, the Germans lost 3,500 prisoners, who reported that their regiments were badly shaken by the vicious fighting.

The AIF 1st and 2nd Divisions were weary, but their morale was high when they were withdrawn. Because of their battle skills, the British line now ran across the western side of the main heights and through Polygon Wood. C.E.W. Bean heard Diggers say cockily, "We could have done it in half the time." Bean knew better. The triumph was the result of careful, methodical planning by the Staff and steady execution by the officers in the field.

The next part of General White's tactical plan called for the "Battle of Polygon Wood", which meant the capture of the entire wood itself, the Butte, Tokio Ridge, and part of what the Germans called their Flandern 1 Line, one of their most important defences. The 4th and 5th Divisions relieved the 1st and 2nd on the nights of September 22 and 23. The 5th, which had enjoyed four months' rest, was given the harder tasks on Flandern 1 Line, the 4th was to take Tokio Ridge, and both divisions would supply troops for the capture of Polygon Wood. As before, the attacks had been practised in the back areas. Meanwhile, scout and liaison officers of the 4th and 5th had been into action with the 1st and 2nd Divisions to study the land. They met their own units as they arrived.

The 15th Brigade, under the dynamic Brigadier General H.E. "Pompey" Elliott, took part in desperate fighting on the right flank on the day before the battle was scheduled to begin. This came about because a German counter-attack had driven back the flank of the British X Corps in Reutelbeek Valley, close to the position from which the right of the Australian line was to begin its advance on September 26. Elliot, whose troops were already in the line, made the generous decision to help the British restore their flank. This took a day's hard fighting on the 25th and not only salvaged the situation for the British but ensured that the attack the following morning could take place.

The guns, which began firing at 5.50 am on September 26, provided the most even, accurate and effective barrage that had ever preceded Australian infantry into battle. According to C.E.W. Bean, it was roaring and deafening and it rolled ahead "like a Gippsland bushfire".

"Our wonderful barrage came down cutting a clean line just ahead of us," wrote Captain T.A. White of the 13th Battalion, 4th Division. "The turmoil of the elements would be minute," he added, "when compared with the belching of thousands upon thousands of big guns supported by a continuous hail from hundreds of machine-guns."

The 4th and 5th Divisions of I Anzac Corps and five British divisions followed the barrage on a 10-kilometre front. The Australians' sector was 2,000 metres wide, broadening to 2,500 metres as they reached the enemy's positions. One of the principal objectives was Polygon Wood Butte, in peacetime the Ypres district rifle range. The butte formed a small plateau from which the Germans dominated the nearby country. The 14th Brigade took the position with relative ease and then moved on to capture its second objective, almost 1,000 metres of the Flandern 1 Line, and a number of strong points. In doing so, they captured 200 prisoners and 34 machine-guns.

The 4th Division's advance further north was immaculate except when machine-guns in pillboxes checked it. During one phase of the attack, men of the 14th Battalion ran into their own bursting shells and, shaken, broke formation and turned back. Captain Albert Jacka of Gallipoli, Pozieres and Bullecourt fame, was at the scene and quickly steadied the men before leading them on again. Yet again his cool leadership inspired others.

The 14th, the AIF as a whole, and the Australian nation suffered a grievous loss that day when Captain Harold Wanliss DSO was killed by a machine-gun which he was trying to locate. Aged 26 when he was killed, Wanliss was an exceptional man. He had been dux of Ballarat College and had studied agriculture at Hawkesbury College. So dedicated was he to Australia's future that he had spent his leave periods studying industries which he believed should be introduced into Australia after the war. His many friends, who included General Monash, had expected him one day to "lead Australia". Lieutenant Colonel J.H. Peck, once his battalion commander, said of him: "Many brave men, many good men I have met, but he was king of them all."

As with the Battle of the Menin Road, dash and gallantry held the Polygon Wood advance together at critical moments. The heroism displayed by Private Patrick Bugden was outstanding. Just 20 years of age, Bugden had joined the 31st Battalion as a reinforcement in March 1917, and at once attracted his mates' attention as a powerful man and a born athlete.

The men of the 31st Battalion had come under fire from forward enemy pillboxes cleverly sited so that the advancing Australians would have to pass between them; the pillboxes' machine-guns fired from flank and rear and caused casualties, including Bugden's company commander. His successor, Lieutenant R. Thompson, located the pillboxes and, short of NCOs, he sent Bugden with a small party to attack them. Bugden silenced the guns with bombs and captured the garrisons at bayonet point, but then he spied a party of three Germans escorting a captured corporal of the 31st to the rear. Bugden made a single-handed charge. He bayoneted one

A duck-board path winds through the eerie desolation of Chateau Wood, described by photographer Frank Hurley as "Once a glorious spot in summer."

A three-kilometre-long plank road for transport was laid through this swampland in preparation for the Menin Road battle.

Young German soldiers ponder their fate the day after capture by Australian troops on Broodseinde Ridge. The Germans sustained enormous losses on what they officially called "the black day of October 4".

German, shot the other two and protected the unarmed corporal as he ran back to the Australian lines.

During the next two hectic days, many stretcher-bearers became casualties and wounded men lay in the mud and under fire. On five occasions Bugden ignored the great danger and rescued wounded men unaided. His luck ran out and he was killed while bringing in a wounded man. When the 31st was relieved, Bugden's mates carried his body back to Hooge Crater cemetery and buried him. His sustained courage was recognised by the award of the VC.

The 4th Division battalions captured all their positions — woods, blockhouses and trenches — but at the high cost of 1,717 casualties. The more heavily engaged 5th Division suffered 5,471 dead and wounded and also took its objectives. Pompey Elliott's 15th Brigade was hit the most severely, with 1,999 casualties. The full loss for the seven German divisions involved was heavy but never known in detail; the 50th Reserve Division alone lost 1,850.

Following the fighting of September 26-28, the way was open for the AIF's third combat of the series, the "Battle of Broodseinde Ridge", a few kilometres south of Passchendaele. Being further back, Passchendaele was not part of the objective at this point. The 1st and 2nd Divisions replaced the 4th and 5th in the front line and were joined by the 3rd, which took over a length of the British line. On the 3rd's immediate left the New Zealand Division came into the line. Never before had four Anzac divisions attacked side by side. They were the centre of a line of 12 divisions on a 13-kilometre front. Their left, or northern boundary, was Gravenstafel Spur, Broodseinde itself was roughly in the middle, and on the right was the village of Molenaarelshoek.

This was the most important of all three battles and potentially the most decisive. When the

British abandoned Broodseinde Ridge after Second Ypres in 1915, the Germans made it their main defensive line. From this long ridge, which was more like the crest of a slope than a ridge, the German Staff and their scores of observation posts viewed virtually the entire Allied salient. Field Marshal Haig wanted the ridge at any price — and the price was the use of the Anzac Divisions, even though Generals Birdwood and White believed that the 1st and 2nd might be worn out. The depleted II Anzac Corps of the New Zealand Division and 3rd Australian, was restored to full strength with two British divisions, but significantly they were not in the order of battle for the Broodseinde attack. Despite their losses so far, the Anzac divisions would break the Germans' line, the British High Command believed. They had by far the most efficient system of supply and communication of all divisions in the salient. Their successes in the battles of Menin Road and Polygon Wood showed how well their units could function.

The assault was timed for the 6 am dawn on October 4. As luck would have it, the German command had planned an attack for precisely the same time, and against the section of front held by the AIF 1st and 2nd Divisions. As a result, October 4 was one of the most memorable days of the war. At 5.20 am, as the Australians lay in shell-holes under a steady drizzle, heavy German shelling came down, to be followed 10 minutes later by a trench-mortar bombardment. About one Australian in seven was hit. The survivors could do nothing but wait stoically for their own barrage which, punctually at 6 am, descended on the ridge.

The Australians scrambled up and moved forward. Simultaneously, lines of German infantry of the 212th Regiment rose in front of them. For just a second the opposing troops were immobile, staring at each other only 30 metres apart. The Australian Lewis gunners fired first, the German soldiers broke and few survived the Australians' bayonet onslaught.

As always, the German machine-gunners resisted powerfully from their pillboxes, and here and there the advancing Australians

An observation balloon used for artillery sighting in Ypres sector soars aloft on October 23, 1917.

wavered. On the 3rd Division's front, the leading companies of the 40th Battalion were held up by no fewer than 10 machine-guns. One gun crew had set up their Maxim on the concrete roof of a stronghouse, and its bullets were smashing into B Company men trying to take cover in shell-holes.

Sergeant Lewis McGee, armed only with a revolver, dashed 50 metres across open, bullet-swept ground, shot some of the gun crew, captured the rest and seized the gun. His act of spectacular daring was seen by many Australians, most of whose lives he had probably saved. McGee reorganised the advance at that part of the battlefield and during the following week he set a fine example of leadership. He was killed in action on October 12 before he could learn of his award of the VC.

On the same section of front, Lance Corporal Walter Peeler, of the 3rd Australian Pioneer Battalion, went into the attack with the 37th Infantry Battalion. His primary task, with his

First Division pioneers shoulder duckboards across muddy wasteland near Zonnebeke. By October 8, 1917, torrential rain had made roads impassable for supplies, ambulance and artillery, but General Haig ordered an attack for the next morning.

Lewis machine-gun, was to protect his comrades against strafing German aircraft. Pioneers were often attached to infantry units for this purpose. But since there were no enemy aircraft Peeler rushed a section of Germans sniping from a shell-hole and killed nine. As the advance continued, he made two similar attacks. Soon after, an officer pointed out a position where yet another machine-gun was causing casualties and checking the attack. Peeler located and killed the gunner and the rest of the crew ran to a nearby dugout. A bomb drove 10 of them out of this shelter and Peeler shot them down. The citation which accompanied his award of the VC stated, "This non-commissioned officer actually accounted for over 30 of the enemy. He displayed an absolute fearlessness in making his way ahead of the first wave of the assault, and the fine example which he set ensured the success of the attack against most determined opposition." The 37th captured 420 Germans and 20 machine-guns, but lost 47 killed and 152 wounded.

At the time, many generals, politicians and, more importantly, the experienced professional observers such as war correspondents, believed that Broodseinde was the most complete victory won by the British and Empire armies on the Western Front. The Canadians' capture of Vimy in April 1917 had been a great victory, but there was no chance that it could have a decisive effect on the war as a whole. Messines, in July, was an outstanding success, but it was only a step in a greater battle. The triumph at Broodseinde presented the High Command at least with the opportunity, perhaps in the spring, of breaking the Germans' hold.

As always, the Germans had exacted a terrible toll. The three Australian divisions lost 6,500 men killed or wounded, 20 per cent of their strength. German casualties were in the order of 25,000 and more than 5,000 troops had been taken prisoner. The German High Command officially recorded October 4 as a "black day".

It now began to rain again, heavily and persistently, and conditions quickly became horrible. Yet Haig insisted on continuing the

On November 1, 1917, Australian soldiers relax outside their billets in Ypres after their exhausting eight-week ordeal. The critically depleted AIF now depended largely for reinforcements on the return of sick and wounded men.

offensive when it would have been better to consolidate his gains. On October 9, the 2nd Division was required to attack a position known as Keiburg Spur, towards Passchendaele. The British division which was supposed to support the Australians turned up hours late, and the 2nd, fighting alone, was driven back. When the British finally arrived, they fought a brave but futile action. The unfortunate episode reconfirmed the AIF's worst fears about going into action with British troops.

Despite the atrocious weather Haig ordered an attack on Passchendaele on October 12. It was made by II Anzac Corps with the 3rd Australian and the New Zealand Division leading the way and the AIF 4th Division in support. Most of the 3rd could not drag itself out of the mud, but some units reached the edge of Passchendaele.

That they got so far was due almost wholly to the efforts of a gallant Australian captain, Clarence Smith Jeffries of the 34th Battalion. East of Augustus Wood, two large blockhouses stopped the centre of the 34th's advance. Assisted by Sergeant J. Bruce, Captain Jeffries organised an assault party and rushed one of the strong points, capturing four machine-guns and 35 prisoners. Then he led his company forward under bursting shells and machine-gun fire that swept along their line. With his company facing annihilation and the whole advance stalled, Jeffries gathered another party, again with Sergeant Bruce and 10 men.

Cleverly using ground cover and pauses in the machine-gun's firing, Jeffries got his party to within storming distance. He gave the signal and his men rushed the post, but the gun swung around at that moment and killed Jeffries. Sergeant Bruce completed the capture. Jeffries, who was 23, was awarded the VC. Every officer of his battalion was killed or wounded that day. His division, the 3rd, suffered 3,000 casualties, while the 4th received 1,000.

Altogether, the five AIF divisions were in the line for eight weeks and in that period suffered 38,093 casualties. This loss produced a crisis of reinforcement which was never resolved.

The AIF was withdrawn from Ypres Salient, but Haig still pressed his offensives. He made eight in all during the Third Battle of Ypres, or Passchendaele, as it became better known. By the time he settled on a winter front line in mid-November, the British and Empire armies had suffered 448,614 casualties since July 31. Haig had captured about 130 square kilometres of territory and his troops had inflicted 217,700 casualties on the German Army. In terms of human loss, therefore, the battle was a victory for the Germans. Also, they had not been forced away from the Belgian coast and their lines showed no signs of breaking. The victory which Haig claimed, on the basis of a strategic ridge captured, had crippled his armies and extended the length of line he now had to defend.

Several Australian and British leaders, military and political, believed that after its losses in the Ypres Salient, the AIF could not achieve in 1918 what it had accomplished in 1916-1917. It had made its name in the lowlands of French Flanders, in several Somme battles and at Bullecourt, before Messines, but it had been severely depleted and the Australian public had twice, by referendum, decided resolutely against conscription.

The AIF, it was predicted, could only survive by feeding upon itself. The service troops from transport and all other rear echelon units would have to become infantry, machine-gunners and artillerymen. The training units would be broken up and perhaps front-line battalions would be disbanded to supply reinforcements for other battalions. According to pessimists, the AIF was unlikely to remain an elite.

Nevertheless, Field Marshal Haig had great confidence in the Australians — much more than they had in him after his insistence on wasting lives in futile attacks after the Anzac victory of October 4. Haig told the Duke of Connaught, to the Duke's surprise, that the Australians were among the best disciplined troops in the British Forces. And to Birdwood he said, "When they are ordered to attack they always do so."

ON MENIN ROAD

Past the ruins of Ypres Cloth Hall, troops set out on the Menin Road for the front line. After leaving the bombed-out city, soldiers marched in silence with ears cocked for the ever-expected roar of a shell; nothing was heard but hobnailed boots on uneven cobbles.

"A land of horror and dread whence few return"

GATEWAY TO HELL

As fighting in the Ypres Salient continued, Menin Road became an avenue and a symbol of sacrifice. Leading from the ancient Flemish town of Ypres, which was encircled by stout ramparts and a moat so that all movement in and out was through great gateways, the road travelled east to the fighting front where the town of Menin, 20 kilometres away, was in German hands.

The most famous of the gates was Menin Gate, where two great stone lions, scarred by shell-fire, stood guard. Behind the walls, Ypres itself was practically demolished, still it provided some cover. Once a soldier passed through Menin Gate he was vulnerable.

The road was the main artery linking the front line to the back areas from which it was supplied. It led to most of the places where the Diggers fought, including Broodseinde, Polygon Wood, Zonnebeke, Westhoek and Hill 60. Just one-and-a-half kilometres out of Ypres was a crossroads called Hell Fire Corner, regarded by troops as "the hottest place on earth". German guns were permanently ranged onto this point and drivers whipped up their horses and men trotted past this notorious spot.

The road itself disappeared under almost incessant shell-fire. For a few months in summer Menin Road was, at best, a rutted track, but during wet and wintry weather it became a plank road. Three-metre-long planks of elm or beech were laid over filled shell holes, cross-planks then were placed next and the road was firmly held by pine logs bolted to the edge.

Hundreds of thousands of soldiers marched up that road, many of them never to return. The names of 55,000 British and Commonwealth soldiers who were never recovered from the Ypres Salient were placed on a modern Menin Gate memorial. It was the loss of those men that etched the memory of Menin Road in the minds of all Diggers fighting on the Western Front.

Above: For their fallen comrades, Australian pioneers fashion crosses of oak from the doors of Ypres' 12th Century Cloth Hall. Below: At a brisk trot, transport drivers pass the notorious "Hellfire Corner", a junction on Menin Road heavily shelled by German guns. Transport wreckage and bloated corpses of horses littered the area.

Above: Uniforms spattered with wet clay, senior 3rd Brigade staff transmit orders by telephone in their cramped, leaky underground HQ at Hooge. The infamous Hooge Crater, a gigantic, waterlogged mine crater, was located nearby and the network of dug-outs completed by the 1st Tunnelling Company had to be constantly pumped free of water. Right: During the Battle for Menin Road, 3rd Battalion troops hold a trench at "Clapham Junction", an advanced mustering point for the attack subjected to intense bombardment.

William Longstaff's grandiose postwar oil painting "Menin Gate at Midnight July 24, 1927" teems with the translucent figures of dead Australia

3 GERMANY'S DEVASTATING OFFENSIVE

A vicious German offensive brought the Allies to their knees. The 1st Division AIF secured Hazebrouck, but the defence of Amiens proved much tougher. Then, in wild, countering attacks around Villers-Bretonneux, the 13th and 15th Brigades stopped the enemy advance.

As the Australians came out of the Ypres Salient battlefield they learned that the 1st, 2nd, 3rd, 4th and 5th Divisions were to become one Australian corps. It had been proposed, by Haig and Plumer among others, that the 4th Division, numerically the weakest of all after its many battles, should be broken up to make good the shortages of men in the other divisions. The 4th now learned that it had been reprieved.

Behind these decisions lay much planning by Generals Birdwood and White and pressure from the Australian Prime Minister, W.M. Hughes, and his Government. Hughes had gone on insisting that the Australian divisions must be brought together. The shrewd White, with Birdwood's concurrence, suggested that Haig should allow the 4th Division to be a depot division, acting as a reservoir for the other four when necessary and fighting when it could.

Even more persuasively, he argued that by using the new Australian Corps on a quiet sector of the front, its divisions could be built up to strength, as could the 4th. Then, when heavy fighting occurred, all five would be ready. Indeed, he pointed out, whichever division

Before a "stunt", carriers get a hot meal to front-line troops in Dyson's "Bringing up the Stew".

suffered the greatest loss could become for a time the depot division. His devious scheme worked to save the fighting 4th, considered by many veterans to be the elite AIF division.

To the Australian Corps, which in military scales was considered one division too small to be called the Australian Army, were added miscellaneous units which had hitherto belonged to other formations. They included the 3rd Squadron Australian Flying Corps and the two Australian siege batteries of heavy guns. The Corps' motor transport became all-Australian. All the British senior officers and staff officers who remained with the AIF were soon to be transferred out of it, other than Birdwood himself.

One of the earliest orders Birdwood gave as Australian Corps commander was that all hats should be worn in the regulation fashion, left side turned up. This overruled Major General Monash's order to his 3rd Division that hats would be worn down all round. It was said that five minutes after the new order was promulgated no one could find a 3rd Division man with his hat turned down. It was as if the Division, which was vastly satisfied to be linked with the other four at last, had been waiting official invitation to perform the change.

At this time the AIF totalled 117,500 troops, about one-eleventh of the total 1,300,000 British and Empire combat troops on the Western Front. During the latter part of the winter of 1917-1918, the Diggers were busy with night patrols in No-Man's-Land of the Lys River valley, with its moors and marshland. Part of this region had been the Nursery of 1916, but that label had passed into legend. Often the Australians encountered German patrols out after the same prey — prisoners for information. In one period, the Australians made 25 raids and captured prisoners on 14 occasions. In the same time, the Germans made 54 raids, obtaining prisoners only on seven occasions. The disparity was no happenstance and said much about the Australians and their tactics.

On their raids, the Australians rarely fired flares to illuminate the battlefield, in contrast to the Germans, who frequently fired them. The Australians, described by friend and foe as "born night fighters", preferred to watch quietly in the dark and take advantage of the enemy flares.

Innumerable small fights occurred. On the night of March 13-14, the scouts of the 12th Battalion, from Tasmania, reported that a German attack was brewing. Soon after, three enemy officers and 60 men approached three posts of the Australian line. It was the type of event that the Australian infantry genuinely loved, and when they found out later that this was a picked German party of storm troopers from Menin, sent out specially to clear No-Man's-Land of Australian patrols, they laughed delightedly. The crack German soldiers came to the Australian wire and were working their way through it when the 12th's guns cut them to pieces. The post's garrisons chased the survivors in panic back to their own lines. Of the 63 attackers, 16 were left dead in the wire and 14 were captured.

That winter, the men in the line often ate and even slept standing in mud. Still, a captain of the 38th Battalion, F.E. Fairweather, wrote home, "In spite of all the discomfort, the hard work and the danger, there was not a single complaint from the boys. They were only too eager to have a decent go at the Boche."

The British line was thinly spread because Haig had taken over an extra 100 kilometres of front from the still weak French. Also, to reduce Haig's potential for ruinous offensives, Lloyd George and the War Cabinet kept back in England the reinforcements which Haig had demanded and sent six divisions to the Italian front. All this time, the German General, Erich Von Ludendorff, was preparing the greatest offensive of the war by moving two divisions a day from the Russian Front, where they were no longer needed, to the Western Front, along with an additional 1,000 heavy guns.

The attack was brilliantly conceived. Ludendorff prepared equally strong armies on three separate fronts, thus deluding Haig and the French commander, Marshal Petain, into

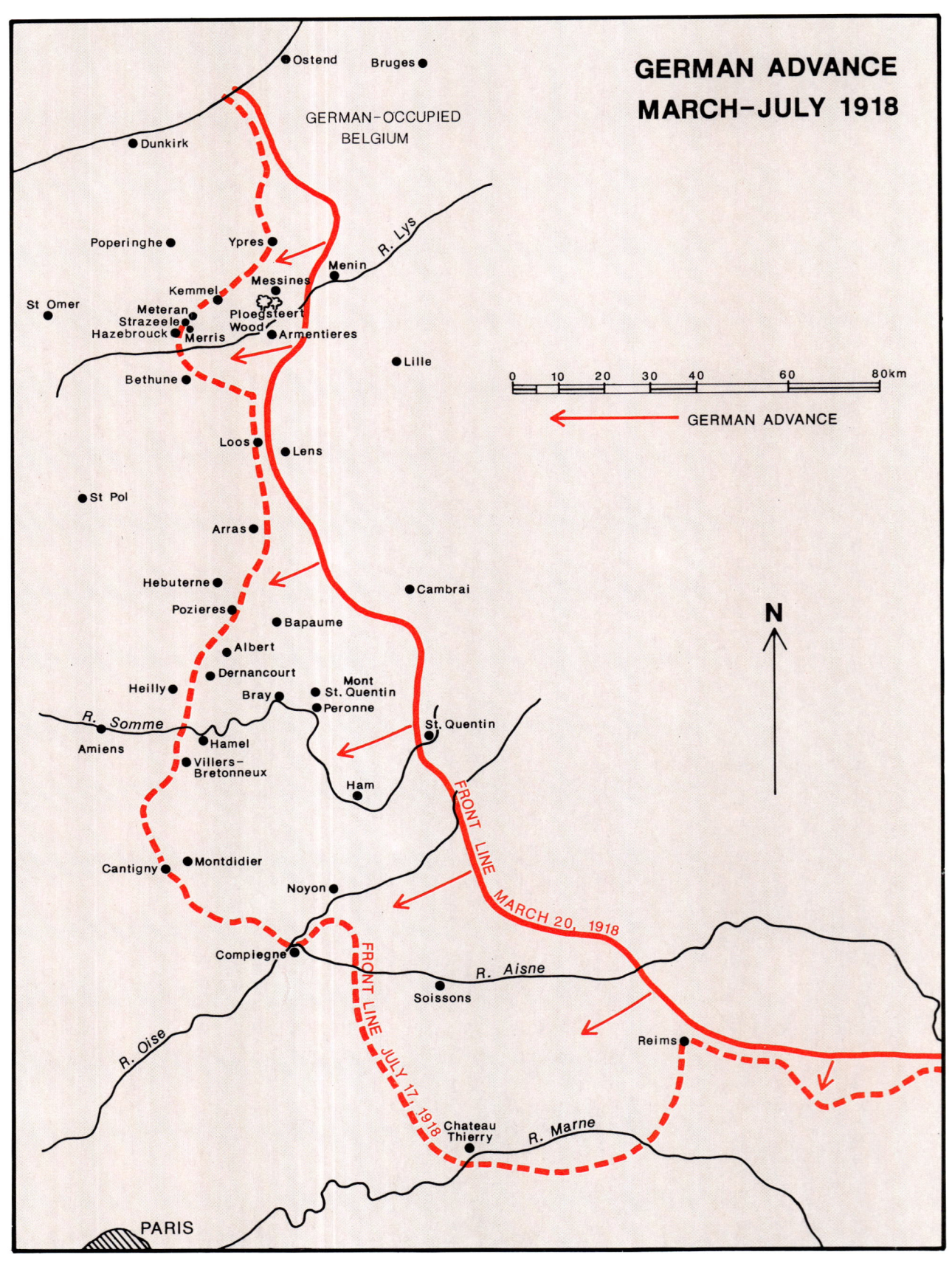

While the Australians kept the enemy on their toes with active night raids, the German General Erich Von Ludendorff was planning a major Spring offensive. He struck on March 21 between Arras and St. Quentin, capturing many of the places previously fought for in 1916, then he took the city of Albert. Ludendorff attacked again in early April in Flanders, but the 1st Division AIF halted the advance at Hazebrouck.

believing that he would spread his forces for a more general offensive. In fact, on every night for three weeks Ludendorff moved large numbers of men to the central of the three fronts. Storm troopers were specially trained and Colonel Brüchmüller, the noted artillery expert, concentrated his guns and howitzers.

The German General Staff knew precisely where to strike — at the junctions of the British Fifth and Third Armies. At dawn on March 21, 1918, Ludendorff unleashed *Operation Michael,* and British troops between Arras and St. Quentin were smothered by a storm of gas shells and hammered by high explosive and shrapnel. Trenches and dugouts were obliterated, whole fields of barbed wire were uprooted and jumbled and few telephone lines remained intact. The Fifth Army took the brunt of the assault and its forward troops suffered heavy losses. Because of fog the defenders who remained at their posts could see nothing until they were overwhelmed. The Germans swept on, bypassing pockets of resistance and creating a gap 65 kilometres wide on the old Somme and Arras battlefields.

Germany's divisional commanders were told that when they broke through they must continue; they were not to expect reinforcement and they must ignore what was happening on their flanks. Nevertheless, the fighting line would be constantly supplied from behind. Within the space of only four days all the British and Empire blood and struggle of the past year went for nought. On the part of the front attacked, the troops were back where they had been at the end of 1916 and the German drive was threatening to spread behind the Allied lines, in the way that floodwater does after breaching a dam.

One hundred kilometres to the north the AIF men at first heard the news without real concern, but when the seriousness of the breakthrough became clear they were eager for action. On March 25, the 3rd and 4th Divisions were on their way to battle by bus, lorry and train. The 4th Brigade lorries rolled into St. Pol and villages around it, where villagers were

General Ludendorff (right) confers with the Kaiser (centre) and General Hindenburg. Ludendorff's Western Front offensive planned for March 1918 was optimistically dubbed "The Kaiser's Battle".

frantically packing their belongings onto farm carts to flee from the advancing Germans. Australian infantry had never been billeted in this area but the French people at once identified them and called to one another, "Les Australiens!" and unloaded their carts.

C.E.W. Bean recorded that an Australian officer asked the reason for their sudden change of plan. "It's not necessary now," an old man told him. "You'll hold them."

Late in the afternoon of March 26, Brigadier General C.H. Brand was ordered to recapture Hebuterne with his 4th Brigade. In the dusk, the 13th Battalion worked slowly through the ruined village, flushing out and fighting the German advance party which had occupied it. Shortly after midnight Brand held the place. To his Australians, who had spent the previous month miserably in the trenches of Flanders, Hebuterne was a paradise. The villagers had fled only a few hours earlier and the remains of their evening meals were on the tables. Fowls and rabbits in the yards were vigorously raided. Several billets were littered with feathers. Somebody found an old French cache of wine, but according to Brand no man became seriously drunk. Some of the men slept in beds and all spent the night in warm shelter. Many of them had not been so relaxed in many months.

The gala atmosphere lasted until next morning. As the sun rose, the 4th saw an amazing spectacle. The countryside east of them — the old Somme battlefield — was teeming with movement as German guns, wagons and infantry approached across the fields. At 11 am, after a barrage, the enemy infantry made their first attack. Shelled by British guns, they went to ground and then crept forward while another wave and then another rushed to the attack.

The 4th Brigade's battalions held firm but, just to make sure that they stayed put, an order came through from the divisional commander, Major General Sinclair MacLagan: "It is to be distinctly understood that no retirement from our present position is permissible. All officers and ranks are to be made to understand this. Most stringent orders must be issued by all commanders to this effect and officers who fail to observe the spirit of this order are to be relieved of their commands."

The Australians, with the New Zealand Division on their right, not only held their positions, they attacked to keep the Germans off-balance. After much spirited action, the 4th was still there a week later and Brigadier General Brand, in a message to his battalion commanders, said: "All the higher commanders would like to see your men get a few days rest, but the holding of Hebuterne is all important. It has therefore been arranged that the 4th Brigade will carry on."

The 4th's fellow brigades of the 4th Division, the 12th and 13th, were rushed to Albert, 20 kilometres south of Hebuterne, to replace a decimated British division which had withdrawn. After a 27-kilometre, night-long march in which not one man fell out, the brigades reached villages north west of Albert, where they heard that Pozieres, Mouquet Farm, Thiepval and other places captured at such tremendous cost in 1916 were again in German hands. The enemy had even captured Albert itself. A British artillery brigadier said to Lieutenant Colonel J.D. Lavarack, chief-of-staff to Major General Sinclair MacLagan, "You Australians think you can do anything, but you haven't a chance of holding the Germans."

"Will you stay and help us if we try?" Lavarack asked. And the brigadier did stay, adding his guns to the Australian artillery.

By now, Major General Monash was bringing into position his 3rd Division, which was new to the Somme. Monash's men were the only units heading towards the approaching enemy. British soldiers, army transport and even heavy guns were mingled with refugees heading west. "You're going the wrong way, Digger!" a British soldier shouted. But a British artillery major commented, "The Australians were the first cheerful people we had met in the retreat."

The 3rd had never experienced any fighting in open country because it had never served outside Flanders. Its idea of a battlefield was of a generally flat area of mud and waterlogged holes, as in Flanders. Therefore it was enthusiastic to be moving to meet the German advanced guard marching on Amiens. The 3rd's brigades had been two nights without sleep but when they climbed down from their transport and faced the early sun on the Amiens road, their fatigue dropped off them. On this lovely spring morning, there before them was a green hillside. Neither rain nor shells were falling, the countryside was clean and the villages were all in one piece. This, somebody said, was the Somme. "It will do me, Digger," said one man, grinning to his mate.

The Australians were moved by the French civilians' embraces, hearty handshakes and smiles of affection and by their implicit trust. Bean recorded one of the most memorable incidents of the period. A village woman approached a Digger as he sat cleaning his rifle while his unit of the 3rd Division halted in Heilly on its way to battle. When she asked him anxiously about the situation he said, "Fini retreat, Madame. Fini retreat — beaucoup Australiens ici."

This might have seemed like bravado to an outsider, but the veteran Australians were reacting with characteristic calm to the panic and chaos around them. With the front unstable, communications inadequate and

After blocking the German advance at Hebuterne, tired 4th Brigade soldiers, transferred south, discuss enemy gains on the Somme.

information unreliable, it was an Australian speciality. A quick decision, even by junior ranks could prevent a serious breach in the still scattered defences, and such a situation developed on the front of the 47th Battalion, which was lining a railway embankment near Dernancourt village. Two gunners with a Lewis gun covered a level crossing and nearby with another two men was Sergeant Stan McDougall, a former blacksmith from Tasmania.

Shortly before dawn McDougall allowed his two men to doze while he continued to watch through the mist. A pair of the 47th's officers on a tour of inspection had just moved on when McDougall heard the sound of bayonet scabbards, slapping on the thighs of marching men. They had to be Germans because the noise came from the other side of the level crossing. McDougall roused his resting men and, hearing his voice, one of the officers called out, "Is that you, Mac?"

"Yes, come up here quickly," McDougall said. "I think they're coming at us."

He ran along the railway to alert his platoon, away to the left, and saw many hundreds of German soldiers looming out of the fog in a steady line and approaching the embankment. As McDougall spaced some men along the embankment, the Germans threw bombs and one of them disabled the two Lewis gunners. Snatching up the gun and firing from the hip, McDougall shot down two enemy machine-gun crews. Firing along the railway, he hit several other Germans. In fact, they belonged to the second wave. About 50 of the first line had crossed the railway and were trying to get behind the men of the 47th Batallion. McDougall's fire killed some and scattered the others. He had badly blistered his hands on the hot barrel of the Lewis, so Sergeant J.C. Lawrence held the weapon while McDougall fired it until he ran out of ammunition.

Two other sergeants closed on the few score Germans remaining on the Australian side of the railway line, but they did not see a German officer step out from a break in the bank and aim his revolver at them. McDougall did. Now armed with rifle and bayonet, he yelled, "Look out behind you," and charged. As he shot dead the officer, the German's revolver shot missed the Australian sergeants. Because of McDougall's decisive action, soon backed by fire from the 47th and adjoining 48th Battalion, the Germans wavered in confusion and then broke and ran, leaving 30 behind as prisoners.

A week later another strong enemy attack occurred at the same place, and again Sergeant McDougall brought a Lewis gun into action in a forward and exposed position, from which he enfiladed the line of Germans. When a bullet damaged his gun he crawled 300 metres under fire, found a replacement and continued the fight. As the 47th counter-attacked, the sergeant's platoon commander was killed, and McDougall led the platoon through the remainder of the action. For his conspicuous bravery and devotion to duty on the night of March 27-28, McDougall was awarded the VC and for his second deed of daring, the Military Medal. His company commander, Captain N.F. Bremner, said of him: "He was a dinkum Digger and a tower of strength."

On March 28, the British 1st Cavalry Division, a hard-fighting formation much admired by the Australians, halted the British retreat in front of the village of Hamel and the town of Villers-Bretonneux, both forward of Amiens. That city, with its vital road and rail junctions, was a great prize and Ludendorff was not prepared to call off his offensive now that he was so close to it. German shelling had ruined the railways so Ludendorff brought up 60 railway construction companies to restore the lines and thus bring in a flow of guns, ammunition and men. On April 4, after a bludgeoning bombardment, he struck with 15 divisions. The northern thrust was stopped by the British 1st Cavalry and the AIF 33rd Battalion. Further south, the Germans reached the outskirts of shell-battered Villers-Bretonneux. If it fell, as seemed inevitable, the way would be open to Amiens.

Brigadier General Rosenthal, commander of the 9th Brigade, had been ordered to stay well

JERRY: A GREAT FIGHTING FORCE

When the Australian troops reached the front in 1916 they had only a vague idea of the Germans as soldiers, and in their ignorance they commonly and confidently agreed that they would "lick the Hun". They also referred to the enemy as "Jerry" or "the Boche".

It was not as easy as they had expected. The enemy army was composed largely of veterans with nearly 20 months' fighting experience, it was ably led at all levels, its equipment was good, and it had been more successful than the Allied armies, so its morale was high. All fighting was taking place on French and Belgian soil and not in Germany, and for this reason the German High Command still believed that it held the strategic and tactical advantage.

The Australians on Pozieres Ridge had at times been frustrated by the absence of Germans to shoot at; they were in the bunkers, in vast, deep dugouts that gave complete shell-proof cover to the bulk of a trench garrison until it emerged to oppose advancing infantry.

The German infantry was taught that while under attack no trench would be left wholly unmanned for a moment; single sentries would stay at their posts even under heavy bombardment. The moment that artillery fire slackened, ceased or passed over a trench, a part of the garrison would man the defences and set up machine-guns. Should they see signs of an assault they would call out the remainder of the garrison.

The German Army was the first military force to realise the profound effect that the medium and heavy machine-gun would have on war. More Australians were killed by machine-gun fire than any other way.

The German Army also tried to keep the initiative in grenade fighting. Germany produced more than 300 million of these weapons during the period 1915-1918. Several types of bomb were used. The famous egg grenade weighed over 300 grams and could be thrown about 50 metres. As the war progressed the well-known stick grenade became the principal bomb. It could be thrown further than the Mills bomb which the Australians used, but was not as lethal. Millions of stick bombs were thrown at Australian soldiers and, in 1918, rifle grenades with a range of 200 metres were fired at them.

German infantry transferred from the Russian front arrive at the Marne salient.

The standard German infantry weapon was the 1898 model rifle, the Gewehr 98, based on a Mauser system, with a 7.9mm calibre and a magazine holding five rounds. German snipers were deadly accurate.

The Australians had first faced German flamethrowers at Bullecourt; by that time the enemy was using a completely portable flamethrower carried on the back.

Although Germany's infantry had been a formidable opponent on the ground, from early on in the war its commanders had been prepared to trade space for enemy casualties. At a certain point in a fight the Germans would retreat from front-line trenches, but still cause the enemy occupiers horrendous casualties. Linked with these tactics were large powerfully built blockhouses, which were really small forts housing machine-guns carefully sited to sweep avenues of approach.

With a long national tradition of militarism, the German army approached the war with a professional air. German officers were intelligent, educated and strict, but the real strength of the German Army lay in its magnificent senior NCOs, who were mainly responsible for discipline but increased their role in action as the shortage of officers became acute. And, although many young Germans were conscripts and did not want to be soldiers, they were brave and determined in attack, and grimly stubborn in defence.

They earned the grudging respect of Australian soldiers who had gone to war fiercely hating the "evil Hun". Most continued to do so, though many Diggers treated prisoners well, and shared water, food and tobacco with them. Australians occasionally risked their lives to tend Germans wounded under fire, and learned that German soldiers also did the same for their comrades. The enemy could be generous and humane, the Diggers discovered, as much as any man facing the horror of an inhumane war.

behind the front, for his own safety, and left Lieutenant Colonel H.A. Goddard of the 35th Battalion in charge of the 9th's troops in Villers-Bretonneux. About 5 pm Goddard learned, to his bitter disappointment, that three companies of his own battalion had retreated in rout. Facing the crisis in a wrecked house in Villers-Bretonneux, he turned to Lieutenant Colonel J.A. Milne of the 36th Battalion and said, "Colonel, you must counter-attack at once."

Milne, a Scot, had been a private in the old British army before emigrating to Australia. Formal by nature and training, he jumped up, saluted and ran to join his troops, in reserve along a sunken road. The 36th already knew the situation was desperate because hundreds of British infantry, having thrown away their arms, had retreated through their lines. "You'd best get out, chooms," one of them shouted. "The Jerries are coming on in thousands!"

Ignoring this advice, the 36th fixed bayonets, spread out below the lip of the plateau in front of them and waited for orders. They urged the retiring British to join them, but the men were spent. Having seen that Monument Farm and the adjoining open plateau was the main danger area and that the German troops were spreading over the country, Milne shouted for his company commanders. His well-remembered verbal order was a model of military directness: "The enemy has broken through in our immediate front and we must counter-attack at once. Bushelle, your company will be on the left. Rodd, B Company will be in the centre. Tedder, C Company will take the right and I shall send immediately to the CO of the Queen's on our flank and ask him to cooperate. Bushelle, your left flank will rest on the railway embankment. Attack in one wave. D Company, under Captain Gadd, I shall hold in reserve here in the sunken road. Get ready. There's no time to waste."

While the attack companies made their final preparations Milne walked along the line. "Goodbye boys," he said. "It's neck or nothing." As the Diggers moved off, Milne's adjutant found Brigadier General Wood, commander of the British 55th Brigade, rallying two companies of the Queen's Regiment. Wood at once sent 180 men into the attack on the flank of the 36th.

At a trot, with bayonets flashing, the 36th passed over the crest and were seen by Germans advancing in waves from Monument Wood, 360 metres away. The pace of the purposeful line of Australians quickened and the Germans, after hesitating, ran back into the wood. The Australians established a long, thin line from which the fight continued intermittently all night. The German offensive had driven the British Fourth Army back on its entire front, in places to a depth of three kilometres, but that the situation did not worsen was due almost entirely to the AIF 9th Brigade and to the British 3rd Cavalry Division, whose horsemen had protected the Australians' flanks and sometimes sallied out to break up assembling German infantry. On April 14, a shell burst in Colonel Milne's HQ and killed him. He had not lived long enough to be rewarded for his outstanding work.

Some senior Australian officers, as well as C.E.W. Bean, considered that one of the strongest attacks made against Australian troops during the war occurred at Dernancourt, almost five kilometres south of Albert. Two AIF brigades, the 12th and 13th, understrength with about 4,000 men in all, were tremendously outnumbered by large parts of four German divisions totalling 25,000 troops.

On the west side of the Ancre River valley, with the advantage of a railway embankment as their defensive line, the Australians held back the swarms of German infantry. From the heights across the valley German artillery put down a heavy barrage of gas and high-explosive shells, not only over the positions held by the two beleaguered brigades but on the back area of the 4th Division.

The 48th Battalion, under Lieutenant Colonel Ray Leane of Pozieres fame, seemed to be at the focus of the enemy attack. Some brave and resourceful German soldiers forced their way under a railway bridge, outflanked the

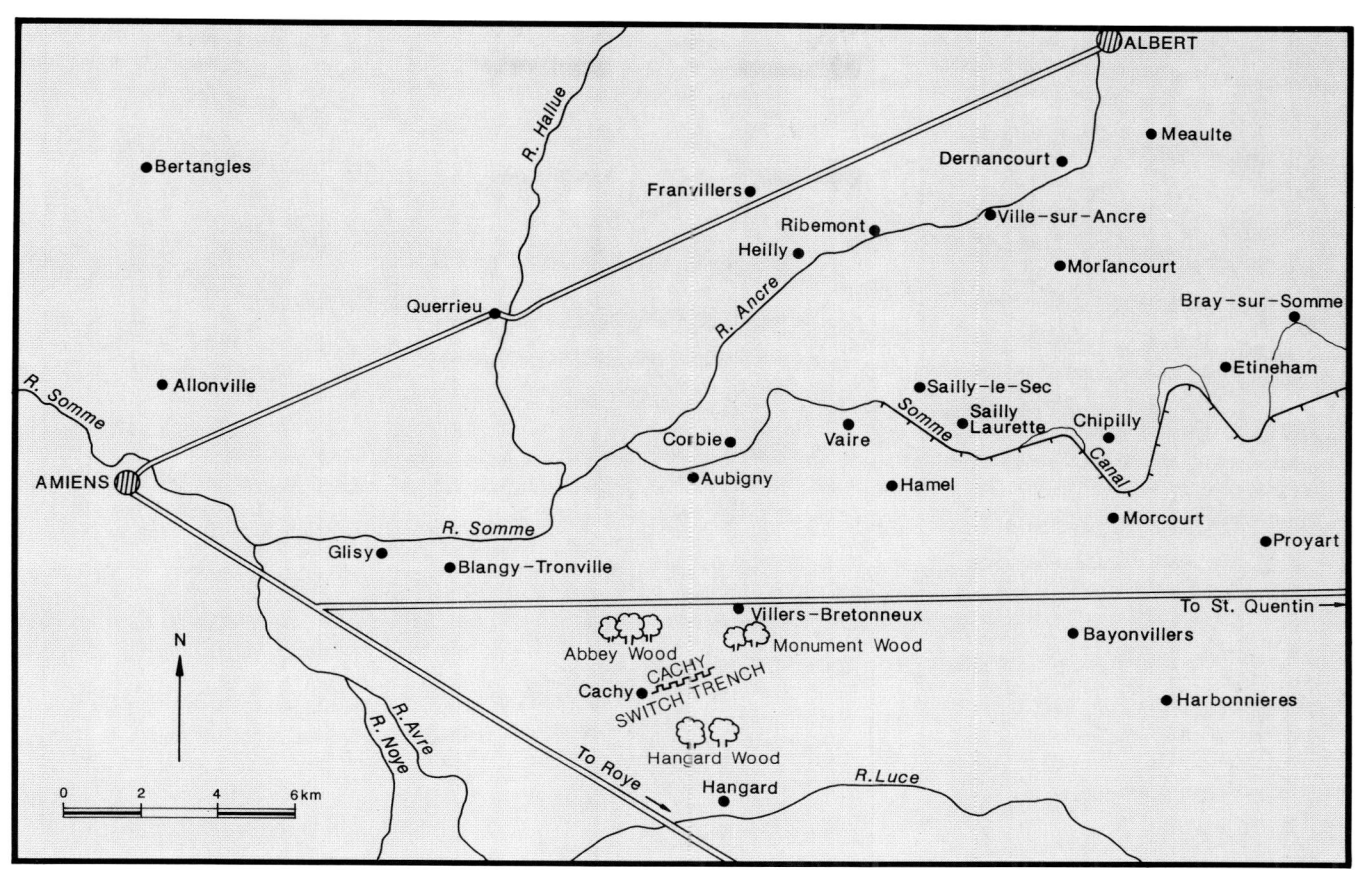

The strategically vital city of Amiens was firmly in the sights of General Ludendorff, but first he had to break through the high ground and woods around Villers-Bretonneux which the Allies considered the key to Amiens' defence. German tanks and infantry easily broke the British lines on April 24, but the AIF's 15th and 13th Brigades entered the battle and forced back the enemy in a series of wild charges.

Australian posts on top of the embankment and dragged a field gun behind the 48th's outpost line. Their infantry followed them. It was Bullecourt all over again. Having beaten the enemy in front, the Australians found them straight across their rear.

The 48th had been ordered to hold at all costs, but at noon, with envelopment and then annihilation imminent, the senior officer remaining, Captain F. Anderson, ordered a withdrawal. Colonel Leane, fighting at another point, would have given the same order. With high competence, the 48th came out successfully, showing a now typical Australian cool pride.

A German war correspondent wrote after this fight, "The Australians and Canadians are the best troops that the English have." Months later, a similar tribute was found to have been paid by German soldiers, who buried a soldier of the 48th at Dernancourt. On a wooden cross they had written with an indelible pencil, *Hier liegt ein tapferer Englischer Krieger.* ("Here lies a brave warrior.")

By April 8, the AIF 1st Division, the last AIF division brought south from Flanders, was moving into support on the Somme. Only three days later it was being rushed back by train to northern France. On April 9, Ludendorff had struck again, this time with *Operation George 1*. It had been planned in November 1917 as a second strike at the British defences should *Operation Michael* not be successful enough to break the line completely. The Germans had chosen the point of their attack carefully. The line across the Lys River valley, south of Armentieres, was held by two understrength Portuguese divisions, which British senior officers considered nothing more than a bait for the Germans. If so, the Germans were only too pleased to snap it up and they gave the task to their entire Sixth Army of four corps.

In fact, the German General Staff was seriously worried that the British would pull the unmotivated, overconfident and unsoldierly Portuguese out of the line before their offensive began. It was a close thing. The Portuguese were due for relief on the night of April 9; the German assault started that morning. The Portuguese fled in panic and many did not stop until they had reached the French coast 80 kilometres away. Among the British units rushed in to plug the gap was XI Corps' Cyclist Battalion; the Portuguese had stolen their bicycles for a faster getaway.

The breakthrough was a disaster for the Allies. On April 10, the Messines positions, taken and held at great cost by the Australians in July 1917, were abandoned. Germans reached Ploegsteert Wood, which had been in the back area, passed north and south of Armentieres, and the British line, already broken on the Portuguese section, cracked in other places. In front of the Germans lay the town of Hazebrouck, through which ran the railway lines which supplied the British front in Flanders with half its daily supplies. In this crisis the Army had practically no reserves left, and on April 11 Haig issued a special Order of the Day, which ended with an exhortation: "There is no other course open to us but to fight it out! Every position must be held to the last man; there must be no retirement. With our backs to the wall and believing in the justice of our cause, each one of us must fight to the end. The safety of our Homes and the Freedom of mankind alike depend upon the conduct of each of us at this critical moment."

A few of the AIF 1st Division did not reach battle, being killed or wounded at Amiens station by German shelling. Some units reached the Hazebrouck area early on April 12, others throughout the day and night. General H.B. Walker, already on the spot, put his brigades into position to cover Hazebrouck. By now, Haig's special order was known to the Australians and it brought them to a pitch of expectation and determination. Most of the men had civilian friends in the towns which they were now passing through. In Strazeele, a village watchmaker handed out his stock of watches to passing Australians rather than have them looted by the Germans.

Throughout the next several days, the Australians held firm against numerous local attacks while more general artillery bombardment reduced many villages to rubble. A shell burst in the 2nd Brigade's ammunition dump not six metres from the sentry, Private T.W. Bratt. It set off other shells in a dangerous and spectacular display of "fireworks". A mature 54, Bratt sloped arms and continued to march up and down on his beat with a display of Digger phlegm which left his sheltering mates astounded. Miraculously unwounded, he stayed on duty throughout the shelling.

The Australians, asked to obtain prisoners for identification, often found them without having to go to the dangerous lengths of a trench raid. On April 18, concealed posts of the 7th Battalion allowed two wandering Germans to pass. The enemy soldiers led a donkey loaded with two large bags of loot from farms in the forward area. At the right moment, the Australians pounced on them. On April 22, two other Germans walked into the 5th Battalion's lines carrying the mail for a unit in their front line. It was a valuable haul for Army Intelligence.

Towards the end of April, after much fighting right along the line from south of Hazebrouck north to Meteran, it was clear that Hazebrouck was safe, and for this the AIF 1st Division was mainly responsible.

Meanwhile, the German High Command was making it evident that the drive to capture Amiens, on the Somme, was far from ended. On the front held by the Australian Corps, scouts repeatedly brought in information that suggested a renewal of the offensive. They reported more enemy wire and new communication trenches, the build-up of transport parks and appearance of heavy guns in new sites. Pilots confirmed the ground reconnaissance reports, and intelligence gleaned from enemy prisoners added to the fear that the next

Soldiers of the 9th Battalion take cover as their billets in the village of Borre, outside Strazeele, are pounded by German artillery on April 17, 1918, during a renewed enemy thrust towards Hazebrouck.

German attack would be a strong one.

The town of Villers-Bretonneux, only 16 kilometres due east of Amiens, was the key to the defence of the city. It was on higher ground with many thick woods around it and it sat astride the railway line. The Australians were not then part of the garrison for the town. That job fell to a battalion of the British 8th Division, a good, well-led formation. However, boys of 18 and 19 made up a large part of its strength; 60 per cent of the 7th Battalion of the Queen's Regiment consisted of boys under 19 and most had never fired a shot. Unlike the Australians, these British youths had received no preparation in a nursery area. The veteran Australians were worried that these "infants" were not yet fully trained. One Digger wrote, "For two days companies of infantry have been passing us on the roads: companies of children, English children; pink-faced, round-cheeked children, flushed under the weight of their unaccustomed packs, with their steel helmets on the back of their heads and the strap hanging loosely on their rounded baby chins."

The 14th Brigade of the AIF 5th Division was responsible for the northern front at Villers-Bretonneux, while the 15th, under Brigadier General H.E. Elliott, was the divisional reserve. However, Elliott was never happy in reserve and kept himself and all his men busy with preparations for battle. He obtained the consent of his divisional commander, Major General J.T.T. Hobbs, to keep a battalion, the 59th, just in the rear behind Villers-Bretonneux. Fearing that the Germans would capture the place, he told its commander, Lieutenant Colonel J.T. Scanlan, to be "continuously prepared" to recapture it. When British troops relieved the 59th, Elliott made another of his battalions, the 55th, his Villers-Bretonneux counter-attack unit. In addition, he ordered Pioneers to build a large-scale ground model of the town and surrounding country and his staff and senior officers were instructed to study it.

In addition to all this, he induced General Hobbs to order the 5th Pioneer Battalion to dig a long trench on his brigade's right flank. It was supposed to be a communication trench, but

A high-explosive shell from long-range German artillery bursts on the quiet streets of Amiens. Fierce random shell-fire rained over the Allied sector for a

...eek prior to the German attack on Villers-Bretonneux.

Elliott intended to use it as a switch or fallback trench to defend his flank if the enemy broke through, as he was convinced they would.

For a depth of several kilometres behind the front, nobody was safe from random shell-fire, but sometimes it seemed to be anything but random. On April 6, two NCOs of the 54th Battalion, Regimental Sergeant Major Bramhall and Sergeant H.H. Kennedy, were standing on the sunken road just behind Villers-Bretonneux when a lieutenant in the grey uniform of the French artillery approached them. He said he wished to speak to the commanding officer.

When Bramhall asked the visitor his business with the CO, Lieutenant Colonel D. McConaghy, he said that his family had lived in Villers-Bretonneux and he wanted permission to visit the house and inspect the damage. He was close by with his battery in Hangard Wood.

"You can go into town," Bramhall said.

"Thank you, but I must have your CO's permission," the lieutenant said.

Bramhall took him to the HQ dugout, where the adjutant, Captain N.B. Lovett and the Intelligence Officer, Lieutenant H.E. Staples, were also present. Written permission was granted and the French lieutenant walked towards the town.

Sergeant Kennedy said to the RSM, "That chap's accent seems more like German than French."

At 3.30 pm, 30 metres of the sunken road where Battalion HQ was situated was shelled. McConaghy, Lovett and Staples were all killed. From the precise nature of the enemy shelling some Australians concluded that the "French lieutenant" was actually a German spy.

On April 21, some German deserters who reached the French lines revealed that German attack preparations were nearing completion. The bombardment would start early on April 24, and for the first two-and-a-half hours would consist of gas shelling. Fifteen new German tanks would take part in the assault. A British pilot came back from low level patrol to report that trenches in Hangard Wood, only one-and-a-half kilometres south of Villers-Bretonneux, were crowded with enemy troops trying to conceal themselves. The Australian guns opened on these positions and hundreds of British guns pounded approach routes and assembly points.

On the night of April 22-23, British and Australian artillery shelled German forming-up areas and the infantry stood ready at dawn. There was no attack, but tension was acute in the British lines and it was heightened even further by aerial activity. Planes from both sides swarmed over the battlefield, bombing and strafing. There were numerous dogfights, and it was during a melee over the Australian lines that the famous German ace Baron von Richthofen was shot down and killed.

On the afternoon of April 23, heavy shelling, mainly mustard gas, fell on the area behind Villers-Bretonneux, signalling the start of the offensive. The whole of Elliott's well-trained brigade stood to arms when the German bombardment fell. Before dawn on the next day, the Germans' monstrous tanks loomed out of the fog at Villers-Bretonneux and a kilometre further south. Wherever they attacked the British line, they broke through at once. Having reached the front trenches unseen in the mist and smoke, they straddled them or came upon them from behind. The boyish infantry panicked at their sudden appearance and, though some groups fought bravely, whole companies were cut off. German soldiers came out of the fog after the tanks and rolled up the British line to the right and left. The Germans took 2,400 British prisoners that day.

Before the sector commander, Lieutenant General R.H. Butler of III Corps, had even heard of the attack, Villers-Bretonneux and Abbey Wood behind it had been lost, as were Hangard village and wood. South west of Hangard the German onrush reached the confluence of the Avre and Luce rivers.

All that morning the staff of III Corps tried to arrange a counter-attack with its British reserves. But except for good work by an advanced gun battery, the most effective response was made by British tanks. In the first tank-versus-tank duel in history, three British Mark IVs fought three German A7Vs. Honours were about even, but it was the German machines that eventually retreated. Australians who watched the duel were spellbound. An aeroplane pilot called up seven British Whippet light tanks to charge German infantry on Villers-Bretonneux plateau. The Germans fled in disorder, but an A7V which had come up put one Whippet out of action. The Whippet commander had no idea that a tank had fired on him; he thought he had been hit by artillery.

While these fights raged within the main battle, Brigadier General Elliott, at his HQ in the village of Blangy-Tronville, paced up and down with mounting impatience and frustration. He was convinced that no formation other than his own brigade was fit to handle the emergency. They should be in action now, yet the Germans were digging in unhindered on the strategic heights facing towards Amiens, and in Abbey Wood. Moving them would be costly.

In mid-afternoon, Elliott was informed that III Corps would recapture Villers-Bretonneux in a pincer's grip, thus cutting off all enemy troops in the town and west of it. His brigade would form the northern pincer and the 13th Brigade, under Brigadier General T.W. Glasgow, the southern one. The 13th, borrowed from the AIF 4th Division, was hurrying down from north of the Somme River.

The commander of the British 8th Division, Major General W.C. Heneker, and his staff were in overall charge of the operation and

A SPECIAL ORDER

In the first few months of 1918, although no major offensive was expected in the Messines sector, it was thought, however, that subsidiary attacks to a coming main assault might occur. In March 1918 the 3rd Machine-Gun Company moved back into the front line of the Ypres Salient at a place known as Spoil Bank, but the position was considered hopeless by Lieutenant F.P. Bethune, the officer commanding No. 1 Section of the Company. It had a field of fire of no more than six metres and if the enemy attacked, the gun crews would be killed almost before they could fire.

Lieutenant Bethune protested to his commanding officer and asked to be allowed to choose other positions. The order remained as it was and Bethune insisted, as a matter of honour, on being in charge of the dangerous post.

As Bethune led his men to the suicide position he was overtaken by a runner who told him that orders had changed; he was to take up better positions at Buff Bank, not far away from Spoil Bank. This was much more to Bethune's liking.

At that time, British and Australian infantry had been in strength near the guns but they were now moved back to prepare for an attack and this left

Lieutenant F.P. Bethune

Bethune's guns dangerously exposed. With the safety of that part of the line in his hands, Bethune considered that his men should have written orders. He issued these instructions:

SPECIAL ORDERS: No. 1 Section, 13.3.18

1. This position will be held, and the Section will remain here until relieved.
2. The enemy cannot be allowed to interfere with this programme.
3. If the Section cannot remain here alive, it will remain here dead, but in any case it will remain here.
4. Should any man through shell-shock or other cause attempt to surrender, he will remain here dead.
5. Should all guns be blown out, the Section will use Mills grenades and other novelties.
6. Finally, the position, as stated, will be held.

F.P. Bethune, Lieut.
O.C. No. 1 Section.

Bethune's battle order was circulated by HQ 1st AIF Division and later by other staffs. In the American forces, then under training on the Western Front, copies of the order were distributed as "an admirable model of all that a set of standing trench orders should be."

Lieutenant Bethune, a minister in civilian life, had not seriously believed that his men might surrender. "They knew that I knew they could not seriously consider such a possibility and so between us we enjoyed in silence the joke that to an outsider might have seemed a little grim," he said.

Bethune and his squad survived their occupation of the post for 18 days, and the position was held.

Australian gas victims, eyes streaming and bodies painfully inflamed, await treatment at an aid-post in Abbey Wood. From April 17 to 24, 1918, the Villers-Bretonneux region was drenched with thousands of German gas shells.

would use a British composite brigade to recapture the lost part of Hangard Wood on the southern flank. Other British troops would follow the Australians to mop up.

Elliott and Glasgow were ordered to report to General Heneker at Glisy, two kilometres west of Blangy-Tronville. They arrived separately. A quiet and perceptive but ruggedly forthright Queenslander, Glasgow immediately saw that Heneker did not have the information he needed about the confused situation, so he and his brigade major drove to the HQ of the two British brigades holding key positions. The brigadiers, brave men but exhausted, were themselves uncertain of the whereabouts of their own and enemy troops.

What happened next was reported by the ubiquitous C.E.W. Bean. A young British staff officer entered the HQ and Glasgow saw that he was "one of those efficient young English Regular Army officers". He was sweating but perfectly collected and competent. Glasgow knew at once that here was the man he wanted.

Taking him aside, he said, "I want to know if you have troops in Cachy Switch Trench, south of the wood. Have you been up there?"

"Yes, I have just come back from there."

"Are your men in it?"

"Yes."

"Can I be certain that they'll hold?"

"Yes, I'm sure they will."

"Well, how about this trench through the wood? Are you there?"

"Yes, there are a lot of men in it."

"Will they hold?"

"I feel sure they will."

"Get someone through to them and tell them to hang on whatever they do. There'll be Australian troops up to them in two hours' time."

As Glasgow returned to Glisy, he came in sight of the new bridges which Australian engineers had built over the Somme River. His brigade was just beginning to cross and he stood and watched them proudly for a few minutes. He could easily pick out the young reinforcements from the veterans. They had all the signs

Villers-Bretonneux appears deserted and derelict in May 1918, but Australian troops are still stationed in the village. By April 27 vicious house-to-house fighting had driven the Germans into the woods to the south.

of young fresh confidence — a brisk step, helmets cocked jauntily, cigarettes in their mouths and some were laughing. The experienced men walked more heavily and resignedly, with helmets square on their heads. They knew what they faced.

Glasgow went on and, having briefed his four battalion commanders, he returned to General Heneker and explained his plan of attack, which was based on a surprise assault, without previous bombardment and striking eastward.

"You can't do it that way," Heneker objected. "The Corps commander says the attack is to be made from Cachy."

Glasgow at once saw the dangerous implications of this. His men would be advancing north east towards Villers-Bretonneux across the German front, not at it, and they would be exposed and easy targets. He was polite but firm in his reply to Heneker. "Sir, it's against all the teaching of your own army to attack across the enemy's front. My troops would get hell from the enemy right."

Heneker resented Glasgow's display of independence. The atmosphere became strained and Heneker several times referred by telephone to the Corps commander. Glasgow went on stressing that he would do what was asked of him but with his own tactics. And, he said, he would start at 10.30 pm. This caused a further argument because Heneker wanted him to start at 8 pm. This Glasgow refused to do because the light would still be too bright at that time and his men would be easily visible. Heneker again called up the Corps commander. Putting down the telephone he said, "General Butler wants the job done at 8 pm."

Glasgow's patience slipped. "If it was God Almighty who gave the order we couldn't do it in daylight!" he exploded. "Your artillery is largely out of action and the enemy is in position with all his guns."

The matter was once again referred to General Butler and Glasgow was asked successively whether 8.30, 9 or 9.30 pm would suit him. Finally he conceded half an hour and said he would attack at 10. It was still too early and as the 13th Brigade assembled south of Abbey Wood it was observed and fired upon.

Elliott had the best of his separate encounter with General Heneker. The forceful Brigadier had already given his orders, and he amended them only when Glasgow, meeting him at 8 o'clock that evening, suggested improvements.

Elliott never failed to consider the welfare of his men, a marked characteristic among Australian officers, and when he found that he had time to spare before the 10 pm start he ordered that a drink of hot tea be served to every man. The AIF had a fixed rule that no alcohol would be issued before an attack because it led to muddled thinking and hasty bravado. When rum was available, it was sent to the troops after a fight, when they most needed it.

Glasgow's 51st and 52nd Battalions were to lead; their orders were to head for Monument Wood and allow nothing to stop them. This necessity was impressed on all officers. Men of the 52nd Battalion passed large numbers of British soldiers who had been ordered back to regroup in safety. "Give 'em hell, Aussie," one Englishman said. "They've knocked us rotten."

As the Australian advance moved confidently in the open, past thick woods, its right flank was abruptly halted by heavy fire from the massed machine-guns of the 4th German Guard Division. Many men of Captain Harburn's company were hit. In command of the platoon most directly under fire was Lieutenant Clifford Sadlier, who was considering a solution to the crisis when he found Sergeant Charlie Stokes, of a nearby platoon, by his shoulder as they hugged the ground. The tall, tough Stokes was every inch a man of action.

"What's to be done?" Stokes asked.

"Carry out the order," Sadlier said. "Go straight to our objective."

"You can't do it," Stokes told him. "We'll all be killed."

"Well, what can we do?" Sadlier asked.

Stokes's advice was that Sadlier should collect his bombers, go into the wood and bomb out the guns. Sadlier agreed with Stokes that a grenade attack on the enemy guns could get the general advance going. He called in some men for a raiding party, and having spotted the position of the nearest machine-gun, ordered his Lewis gunner to fire on it.

Meanwhile Sergeant Stokes brought up a bag of bombs. On Sadlier's order the party charged into the wood, firing as they went. The vigorous rush took the Germans by surprise and, unsure of the Australians' exact positions in the dark, they fired wildly. A German who shouted "Kamerad!" nevertheless fired his rifle, wounding Sadlier in the thigh. Sadlier shot him dead with his revolver, and passed onto the next post, which he captured, and the next, where he was shot again. Disabled, he was forced out of the action, but Stokes finished the job. He silenced all the guns in the wood and the brigade completed its tasks only an hour late. Some time after, when his company was held up by barbed wire protected by machine-guns, Sergeant Stokes attacked several of them and took them out one by one.

Both Sadlier and Stokes were recommended for the Victoria Cross, but only Sadlier received it. Stokes was awarded the Distinguished Conduct Medal, although he deserved the VC as much as any of the 65 Australians who were awarded it.

For its part, Elliott's 15th Brigade made a swift rush in bright moonlight north of Villers-Bretonneux and here too there was high drama. Captain E.M. Young of the 59th Battalion was positioned with his company on the edge of orchards near the town. In the light made by a burning house, he noticed Germans in the open and saw an opportunity to strike a decisive blow. He gave the order to charge. In wild excitement the Australians set off in extended line with bayonets levelled. Companies of the 60th Battalion, adjoining the 59th, who were on a different mission, joined in without orders.

Sergeant R.A. Fynch reported: "With a ferocious roar and the cry of 'Into the bastards, boys,' we were down on them before the Boche realised what had happened. The Boche was at our mercy. They screamed for mercy but they had too many machine-guns for us to show them any consideration as we moved forward. The night was turned into day by the numerous enemy flares and the Germans opened a terrific machine-gun barrage, but only in few instances did they put up a fight. Each Australian was in his glee and old scores were wiped out two and three times over."

WHO KILLED THE RED BARON?

Baron Manfred von Richthofen, the 26-year-old "Red Knight of Germany", had wreaked enough havoc on Allied air and ground forces. He had flown over the hottest front lines in France and had become the leading air ace of the war with a tally of 80 victims. The "Red Baron", as he had become known to respectful Allied forces, was not to be taken lightly; even after he was shot down and killed in his bright red Fokker tri-plane, DR 1, over Australian lines on April 21, 1918, his name continued to be a controversial point of debate. A dispute raged over who actually brought him down.

During a dogfight on that spring morning, von Richthofen swooped on a Canadian pilot of 209 Squadron RAF. Coming to the rescue, Squadron commander Captain Roy Brown, a Canadian ace with 11 victories, dived his Sopwith Camel toward the fray and fired a long burst from his Vickers machine-guns into the Fokker. For a full minute later the German ace of aces continued to follow his prey, firing bursts from his own machine gun before crashing close to the Bray-Corbie road, on high ground above the Somme River.

Nearby, Australian gunners manning their posts by the Somme Canal had watched the action unfold before them. Several of them had also fired at the Red Fokker; one was Cedric Popkin of the 24th Machine-Gun Company, 4th Division. After Brown had dived, fired and turned away, Popkin fired 80 rounds in two bursts at the Baron's tri-plane as it flew only 60 feet above him. Soon after, AIF anti-aircraft Lewis gunners Privates Snowy Evans and Robert Buie, both from the 53rd Battery, opened up at close range. Buie was convinced that he had hit the pilot, while Popkin was sure his fire had caused the enemy plane to crash.

Two autopsies carried out on von Richthofen to determine how he had died found that he had been hit by one bullet in the back which then penetrated his heart. The first group of surgeons said the bullet could not have come from the ground, but the second investigation agreed that the bullet had come from ground fire.

It was unlikely that Captain Brown killed the Red Baron. With a bullet through his heart, the pilot could not have controlled his Fokker and fire his guns for a full minute before his crash. During this time the tri-plane was fired at by soldiers from all directions. The strongest evidence suggests that the Australian sergeant, Cedric.Popkin, fired the bullet which killed the brilliant but deadly Red Baron. The Canadians and the RAF, keen to claim the scalp of the war's most famous flyer, were however never fully convinced.

The famous Red Baron, Manfred von Richthofen, was Germany's top-scoring ace pilot.

*Above: An Australian firing party gives full military honours to their respected opponent at the Red Baron's funeral.
Left: A soldier stands guard over the wreckage of Richthofen's Fokker triplane which is eagerly inspected by Australian airmen at their aerodrome near Bertangles. Souvenir hunters had stripped the aircraft shortly after it crashed into Australian lines at Vaux-sur-Somme.*

In C.E.W. Bean's assessment, the charge at Villers-Bretonneux ranks among the "wildest" in the experience of Australian infantry. The men's ferocity was understandable, especially among the veterans. They had often been mauled by German machine-guns without an opportunity to hit back and they had lost many mates. Now, determined to save a town which had become important to them, they had their chance. But it did not go all their own way. A machine-gun crew firing from beside a haystack threw flares to keep the Australians illuminated and shot down a number of them until a lone Australian, Private D. Hodgekiss, circled behind the haystack and killed the gunner. Officers and NCOs regained control of their men and the attack went on as planned.

As the dawn came up on the third Anzac Day, the Australians in Villers-Bretonneux were engaged in a fight from house to house and cellar to cellar, and survival depended on shrewdness and quick action. They captured and held the town during the afternoon. All in all, they thought it an excellent way to celebrate Anzac Day. The capture of Villers-Bretonneux was not considered complete, however, until April 27, when the AIF 60th Battalion straightened the Australian line beyond it, a task which cost them 90 casualties.

One more mission remained: the capture of Monument Wood, which the battered Moroccan Division had failed to secure in a suicidal daylight melee the previous day. Because it overlooked Villers-Bretonneux, its seizure was regarded as important and the difficult job fell to the 12th Brigade. Since its leader was on sick leave, command fell to Lieutenant Colonel Ray Leane, famous for his gallant command of the 48th Battalion at Pozieres in 1916 and Bullecourt in 1917. Leane used his own battalion as his striking unit and on the night of May 2-3 the attack went in. Despite some courageous fighting and the loss of 12 officers and 143 men in the 48th Battalion, only part of Monument Wood was recaptured.

The encounter was most memorable for an episode in No-Man's-Land when Australians walked out unarmed in broad daylight to bring in their wounded. A big German officer misunderstood this action and, climbing out of his trench, he shouted, "Do you want to surrender?"

"Surrender be fucked!" scores of Australians bellowed.

The German said, "I do not understand French. Talk in English."

Lieutenant H.F. Mitchell met the young German in No-Man's-Land and made arrangements for a 40-minute truce. After the dead of both sides had been buried and the wounded removed, Mitchell and the German saluted each other, dropped into their trenches, and the war continued.

In Second Villers-Bretonneux, the 8th Brigade suffered 188 casualties, the 14th, 346, the 15th, 455. The 51st Battalion, 13th Brigade, alone lost 365 officers and men, chiefly in skirting Abbey Wood, where Lieutenant Sadlier had prevented even worse casualties, and in passing some wire barriers. Several machine-gun units were badly hit; the 5th Machine-Gun Battalion lost five officers and 90 men. More than 500 casualties were due to gas. Three British divisions involved in the battle lost 9,849 officers and men, the gallant Moroccan Division 3,500.

The Germans had lost Villers-Bretonneux but little else. Their losses did not exceed 10,000 and by some estimates were only 8,000. As usual, Allied losses were considerably higher than those of the enemy. Once the German troops, with their apparently limitless supply of Maxim medium machine-guns, settled into position, they took tremendous toll of the attacking infantry. In any case, the Germans no longer attacked frontally in waves, as the British and French still did. Under Ludendorff's insistent direction, the major infantry tactic was infiltration. German units wormed their way through the Allied lines or invited attack, allowing their enemies to pass through, and then setting upon them from the rear.

British and French commanders were generous in their praise for the Australian counter-attack at Villers-Bretonneux. Brigadier

A scarred but elegant country house outside Villers-Bretonneux serves as headquarters of 4th Division reserve battalions for the attack on Monument Wood on May 2, 1918. The attack, poorly supported by artillery, had limited success.

General Grogan VC, who saw the action, described the successful counter-attack by night across unknown and difficult ground, and at a few hours' notice, as "perhaps the greatest individual feat of the war". The Allied Supreme Commander, Marshal Foch, referred to the "altogether astonishing valiance" of the Australians. His made-up word was somehow even more appropriate than valour, which he probably intended.

Several officers claimed credit for the success, including Haig, General Rawlinson, commanding the British Fourth Army, and General Butler, commanding III Corps. The officer who pressed his claims least of all, Brigadier General Glasgow, deserved the greatest praise. Had he not stubbornly insisted on the attack being delayed until 10 pm, it would have been a calamity. In any case, the plan for his 13th Brigade was his alone, and played the major part in the town's recapture.

Field Marshal Haig now switched the front of III Corps and the Australian Corps so that the Australians held the front from Villers-Bretonneux north to the Ancre River. This concentrated the Australian infantry under its Corps commander, General Birdwood, except for the 1st Division, which was still in action to the north in the Lys River valley. Placing Australian brigade commanders under British divisional and corps commanders had not been a success at Villers-Bretonneux. The Australian brigade commanders were too independent and sometimes too impetuous for operations under the direction of the more formal and less enterprising British officers. The Australian divisional commanders knew how to handle their strong-minded brigade leaders.

The continued losses of men and the lack of trained reinforcements forced a radical change in AIF organisation. Three battalions had to be disbanded to maintain their fellow units. The

German soldiers charge through a smoke screen, flinging their stick grenades into French positions outside Villers-Bretonneux on April 4, 1918. Despite

initial gains, Ludendorff's offensive had lost momentum by the end of April and exhausted his army stretched across a wide front.

36th went from the 9th Brigade, the 47th from the 12th Brigade and the 52nd from the 13th Brigade. British brigades had earlier been reduced to three battalions, but the decision about the Australian units had worried Birdwood as well as the Australian generals.

All were embarrassed by having to disperse men who had become tightly bound by shared hardship and sacrifice and who had developed immense unit pride. Also, they were worried that the disbandment might cause unrest and even mutiny. The Australian Defence Department objected to disbandment because each battalion now had its own tradition. To disband an Australian battalion was to destroy it.

A compromise was reached. The names and numbers of the three battalions were allotted to Australian training units in England. Also, their assistant adjutants and their quartermasters were posted to these units to provide some continuity of tradition. The battalions' records were sent to the Australian War Records Section in London for protection. On top of all this, the commanding officers of the disappearing battalions explained the decision to the men. Originally most were distressed and many were angry, but the officers and NCOs set a good example by pointing out that what mattered most was the well-being of the AIF as a whole.

In the end the men marched quietly away to enrich their new units with the tradition of their old ones. Each of the disbanded battalions, though young in terms of AIF history, had created a name for itself. The 36th had made a dramatic and splendid charge at First Villers-Bretonneux. The 47th had performed brilliantly at Messines and had twice attacked at Dernancourt. The 52nd, with great courage, had reached and held its objective at Mouquet Farm, Pozieres, and now had an even more illustrious battle honour in the decisive Second Villers-Bretonneux.

At this stage of the war, the effective Allied forces on the Western Front had decreased to 173 divisions, while German strength had grown to 206. Of the Allied divisions, 103 were French and many of them were weak; 52 were British and Imperial; 12 Belgian, two Italian and four American. On May 1, the Allies had 57 divisions in reserve, the Germans 64 and this number was expected to increase to 84.

Much depended on the Americans. They had been at war more than a year since April 2, 1917, but still only four divisions were in France, and only one in the front line. The vast armies being trained in the United States were needed urgently. At the end of April, American help was little more than a promise. In the meantime, the British not only enlisted scores of thousands of boys but raised the military age to 50 and in some cases to 55. As well, two complete British divisions and 23 assorted battalions were on their way from Palestine, where General Allenby no longer needed them.

The Western Front became noticeably quieter — except where the AIF 1st Division was operating. The situation, however, was still critical for the Allies. As for the men of the AIF, they wondered where the next hammer blow would fall, and which side would deliver it.

OUT OF THE OLD KIT BAG

A box-respirator gas mask, with anti-tear-gas goggles and breathing apparatus attached by rubber hose to a filter unit, was worn in a bag on the chest. The surgical field dressing contains bandages and an antiseptic pad. The gas alarm rattle was loud enough to be heard above the roar of battle.

ARMY ISSUE

Army issue kit and uniform equipped the infantryman with the bare minimum for fighting and living in the trenches, but if an Australian wanted something extra he was able to barter and buy whatever he needed to supplement or replace his kit.

Despite the standardisation of army equipment, the AIF soldier always managed to stay unique. Most distinctive was the Digger's uniform. The workman-like woollen khaki jacket, cut loose-necked and baggy, and detailed with dull blackened metal buttons, topped sturdy, lace-up, ankle-length boots made completely of leather and hobnailed for extra grip. Puttees were long strips of woollen material bound round the lower leg from ankle to knee and were intended to stop water and mud sloshing into boots and breeches. They were cursed by soldiers as worse than useless; they cut off circulation when too tight because they shrank in the wet, and unwound when too loose, hampering movement. The rabbit fur-felt slouch hat with its Rising Sun badge became the readily identifiable symbol of Australian soldiery, and when the AIF arrived in France their hats were reluctantly swapped for British steel helmets. In France the Australian soldier was also issued with a wet-weather "gas" cape as worn by the British. Spare uniform, standard kit and a few personal items were packed for travel in a kit bag, a drawstring, light canvas dufflebag with the soldier's name and number stencilled on the outside.

As well as carrying identity papers, the Australian soldier wore two engraved oval ID discs, called "dead meat tickets", on necklets. It was the unenviable job of the Graves Registration Unit to recover these discs from the bodies of the dead to identify those killed in battle.

Left: An ID disc belonging to Sergeant Lowdon shows his serial number, religious denomination (Church of England) and battalion number. Two ID discs were worn around the neck; if a soldier died one was kept on the body as identification for burial and the other was returned to his family. Right: Kitbag, hobnailed boots, puttees and British steel helmet were standard army issue for infantrymen on the Western Front.

INTO BATTLE

An Australian or British soldier's standard piece of fighting equipment was his Lee-Enfield rifle with attached bayonet. Most of these weapons were manufactured in Britain, although a small arms factory in Lithgow, New South Wales, also supplied Australian troops embarking for France with the same rifle. Apart from his Lee-Enfield slung over his shoulder, all the kit a soldier needed for the battlefield was fitted into pouches or hooks on a complex webbing harness that he buckled over his jacket. An entrenching tool, consisting of a wooden handle and detachable iron head (pick-shaped at one end and shovel-shaped at the other), hung from his belt. Field compass, map case, dixie can, mess utensils, water bottle, pocket watch and field dressing were either slotted into pouches or tied to the harness, and were all standard British Army issue. Box-respirator gas masks, which had superseded the more primitive cloth-hood type by mid-1916, were stored in a small haversack hung round the neck at chest level.

This basic survival kit was supplemented in various ways. A family farewell gift often consisted of a practical item like a mesh-covered wristwatch or a brand new pistol. A grisly repertoire of weapons for hand-to-hand fighting — knives, daggers and trench clubs — was either purchased from locals or other Allied soldiers, or confiscated from enemy prisoners. Luger pistols were popular with the officers.

Organisations such as the YMCA, the ACF and the Red Cross sent the troops "comfort" packages. They included writing wallets with paper and pencil; toiletries such as soap, razor blades, combs and shiny, unbreakable, metal mirrors; sewing kits, called "Hussifs"; and enamelled tins containing candles and matches.

Left: A field-service notebook belonging to 20-year-old Australian Private Alan Howard Kilminster (pictured behind) recorded the soldier's last entry, for a cricket match to be played with friends on leave. The notebook, worn in his breast pocket, failed to stop a fatal bullet from a German sniper at the battle of Goncourt, on the Somme, just days before the scheduled match. Right: The map is regular army issue; the field compass was issued to an officer leading a patrol. The pistol was probably a parting gift for a young officer, and the knuckle-duster knife, American in design, was doubtless purchased at the Front.

Left: A stretcher-bearer's brassard, worn above the left elbow, identified him to friend and foe. The small field dressing contains two bandages for light wounds. Above: The mesh-protected wristwatch is a personal farewell present. The wallet and shiny, metal mirror are YMCA Christmas "comforts" gifts.

The "Hussif", known as the "Housewife", (left) was a compact, cloth sewing kit that could fit into a pocket. "The Soldier's Friend" was a hinge-lidded tin which held matches and a candle and a built-in candle holder.

The metal mess tin and blue enamelled waterbottle, with webbing cover, are both army issue. The non-regulation fork was either purchased or "scrounged". The earthenware rum jar, marked "Service Rum Dilute", was delivered to front-line troops for a calming tot after battle.

SOUVENIRS

The Australian soldier earned a reputation as a zealous, if indiscriminate, souvenir hunter. One observer noted that, "As each Hun advanced with his hands over his head, several of our lads would dive at him and, before the Hun knew what was happening, hands were in every pocket and he was fleeced of everything except his name and his clothes."

Before the war, Flanders was a flourishing textile area and the locals soon turned their skills to profit during war time. Silk-embroidered postcards became enormously popular with the troops and they were soon being designed on specific themes: "To Mother", "To Father", cards with AIF colour-patches, national flags, and local sights such as Albert Cathedral and Ypres Cloth Hall were favourites. Silk-embroidered cushion covers, so popular with the troops in Egypt that the Melbourne Singer sewing machine company exported machines to meet the demand, were also made in France with appropriate motifs.

During rest periods behind the lines, bored soldiers indulged in the hand-tooling of exploded shells as gifts of gratitude to nurses or as souvenirs for their families back home. They fashioned all manner of strange items from brass shell casings and bullet cartridges: vases, belt buckles, pots, model planes and tanks and even coffee pots and sugar bowls. German POWs were also encouraged to make "shell-art" for which they received extra rations. Souvenirs categorised as "Zeppelin art" were made from the wreckage of crashed planes, reconnaissance balloons and Zeppelins. They were quickly stripped for metal parts which wound up as tasteful gifts ranging from hat pins to engraved "sweetheart" bracelets.

Left: Two examples of the thriving French trade in postcards for the troops. The silk-embroidered postcard (top) was envelope-shaped; the front flap was hand-stitched with message and motif and a private note was popped inside. The "dirty" postcard, featuring scantily clad or nude women, was rarely sent home. Right: A brass coffee pot, sugar bowl and scoop make a striking ensemble of "shell art". The model plane, about 100 cm in length, is built from a bullet cartridge and shell fragments.

4 TURNING THE TABLES

Having halted the Germans, Australian soldiers further destroyed the enemy's morale with terror-filled raids into No-Man's-Land. Under Monash's command, the AIF turned its next major battle into a model for future successes. The Allies were finally on the offensive.

In Dyson's "Back at Mouquet Farm" a veteran of Flanders returns to the bloody battlefields of 1916.

In February 1916, Brigadier General John Gellibrand, commander of the 6th Brigade, had suggested that the veterans of Gallipoli's Anzac Cove should wear some distinguishing mark. He proposed an embroidered gold "A" to be stitched to the colour patch. The practice originated in the 2nd Division, and in 1918 it was widespread.

By then, the great majority of the 120,000 AIF men serving on the Western Front had not been at Anzac, and the golden "A" was a proud and relatively rare mark of service. It was an indication of the importance the AIF attached to its veterans. Apart from the Anzac insignia, other symbols marked out the veteran. On the right sleeve he wore a chevron for every year of service; red for 1914 and blue for each subsequent year. Even more important was the gilt chevron which indicated a battle wound. Some men — not all of them veterans by years of service — wore four and five such chevrons. A very few wore six.

The groups of reinforcements which reached the battalions from training camps regarded the hardened warriors with great respect. C.E.W.

Bean believed that the veterans had a stronger influence on the young, semi-trained Australian recruits than any factor "since they left their mothers' knees". The senior soldiers were natural leaders because they knew the army, they understood war and they had the confidence of older years and experience. Well aware that they were members of the only fully volunteer army on the Western Front, the Australians carried themselves proudly and gave their respect to no man unless he had earned it. This attitude was particularly strong among the "originals", those men who had been with their battalion since its foundation. "I'm an original" was a demand for respect and for the right to be critical. It was also an inverted way in which the veterans indicated that the number of originals was falling rapidly and that with each battle their own chances of survival were increasingly slim.

Captain R.J. Henderson of the 13th Battalion expressed the feelings of many Australians when he wrote in April 1918, "A few years of this and one treats life very cheaply. Lately some of our officers have been killed who landed with the Battalion on April 25, so that apparently it is only a matter of time. One must look at this game from a philosophic standpoint."

That standpoint was fatalism, according to Lieutenant A.W. Mann of the 25th Battalion, who wrote home during the same period: "You can't stop a shell from bursting in your trench. You can't stop the rain or prevent a light going up just as you are halfway over the parapet. So what on earth is the use of worrying? So smile, damn you, smile."

A mixture of pride and fatalism had much to do with the Australians' military activities after they had stopped the German offensive of March 1918. With zest and vigour they turned to what was wryly called "peaceful penetration". The term was a pre-war one, much used by British and Empire journalists and politicians to describe the insidious creeping tactics the Germans were using in their drive for empire. It was not necessary for the Germans to go to war, the cynics said, because they were taking over the world by peaceful penetration, economic blackmail, undercover political deals and ruthless elimination of local opponents.

But in 1918 there was nothing peaceful about the Australian penetration of German positions. The 1st Division, still blocking the Germans in French Flanders, and the four other divisions 100 kilometres south on the Somme, struck sharply into German-held French territory with the idea of terrorising the enemy and destroying his morale. It was to be raiding on an intense and incessant scale.

The first such operation was led by Corporal D.A. Sayers of the 58th Battalion on April 5, when, with a few men, he cut off and captured a German patrol of an officer and 30 men near Hamel, south of the Somme. Thereafter the battalions engaged in a spirited competition to see which of them could capture the greater number of prisoners for interrogation.

Monash's 3rd Division was particularly successful in peaceful penetration, capturing prisoners on three days out of every five. In the 41st Battalion, the capturing of Germans developed into an unofficial company competition, with B Company the winner. In one exploit, Lieutenant R. Tredenick's patrol rushed a post, killed nine enemy and dragged back two survivors, without loss to themselves. Having any of your own men killed or wounded was considered unprofessional.

Away to the north, on the Hazebrouck front, the 1st Division applied so much verve and skill to peaceful penetration that it approached a fine art. At no time and on no other front was it so successful or continued for so long. For the Germans facing the Australians of the 1st Division it was a period of unrelieved tension.

Some raids were carried out in full daylight. Near Merris, on May 5, Corporal J. Lean of the 4th Battalion saw a single German behind a hedge and crept out alone to capture him. During this action, he saw another post manned by several of the enemy but they did not see him. Having returned and handed over his prisoner, Lean took two men and rushed the enemy post from the rear. One German was bayoneted, but survived and the three others were brought back. Silesians of the 62nd Regiment, they revealed under interrogation that the Germans on this front were unsettled, so the British artillery was ordered to increase its harassing fire and unsettle them even more.

The Australians' tactics were assisted by the Germans themselves. The enemy had manned their trench line with poor quality divisions, while assembling and resting their better units in the back area for pending offensives. Also, the front units were not allowed to defend their positions with barbed wire, since Ludendorff wanted the Allies to believe that his great offensive was only in abeyance, not concluded.

A German in the outpost line wrote about this period, in a letter captured by raiders: "We have the Australians opposite us and they are very quick and cunning. They glide about in the night like cats, and come right up to our trenches without our seeing them."

One of the greatest successes of peaceful penetration took place on the Morlancourt front, south of Albert, as the result of a young officer's enterprise. While making his rounds, Lieutenant A.W. Irvine, Intelligence Officer of the 17th Battalion, found all the Australians manning a length of trench asleep in the sun. Even the sentry was only half awake. It occurred to Irvine and his sergeant, P.J. Boyce, that the Germans would also be asleep. The following day, May 18, Irvine again went to his front trench and was informed by the sentry, "The Huns haven't thrown any tins over for an hour."

This told Irvine that in the noonday heat the Germans were asleep. Australian snipers had prevented them from using their regular latrine, so they relieved themselves in a bottle or tin and tossed it forward. Irvine decided on an instant, silent raid. He should have asked permission from brigade HQ but there was not time; in any case, he knew he had the support of his own commanding officer.

Irvine needed 18 men, but so many volunteered that he had to select his party, to which he added two Lewis gunners for covering fire if needed. Spacing his men two paces apart, Irvine ordered, "Go for the German post in one line. Don't fire, just use the bayonet. We are going to advance at a walk and then a trot." The preparations had taken him only 10 minutes.

As the Australians closed to within 20 metres, a German who had been leaning against the trench side, smoking a cigarette, spotted them. The cigarette fell from his mouth and he held up his hands without a word. The only other German who was awake found a bayonet at his throat and blurted out in English, "Good morning." A digger threw a grenade into a dugout, killing four Germans; the other 22 in the position surrendered. Irvine was back with his prisoners and their weapons within another 10 minutes. News of the audacious raid spread throughout the Australian Corps and beyond, and General Birdwood joined in the praise.

The Australians did not have it all their own way. One setback, known as the Allonville disaster, was caused by Australian prisoners giving away too much information. By international convention, a captured soldier was obliged to reveal nothing more than his name, rank and number. If the enemy could induce him, by clever interrogation, to give away more, then that was their good fortune. In this case, some captured Australians were duped into disclosing that the 3rd Division's HQ was at Allonville, a brigade HQ was at Franvillers and a camp was situated at La Houssoye, all in the Somme.

By the night of May 30, the 3rd Division HQ had been replaced at Allonville by 4th Division HQ with part of the 4th Brigade. Two companies of the 14th Battalion were quartered in two vast barns. That night, German artillery opened on Allonville with high-bursting shrapnel shells. A German pilot, spotting for the gunners, signalled that their shells were on target and they changed to more destructive high explosive. One barn was hit and collapsed. A single burst killed 13 men and wounded 56, the most costly single loss to artillery in AIF history. The next shell smashed through the roof of the adjoining barn, killing five and wounding 12.

An unarmed and terrified German soldier, kitbag slung at his side, surrenders to an Australian daylight patrol that slipped stealthily into enemy lines. As keen souvenir hunters, the Australians quickly relieved prisoners of their possessions.

Hidden in a farmhouse in Ville-sur-Ancre, a heavy trench-mortar crew fire onto German lines only 360 metres away. The village was captured in an Australian operation on May 22, 1918.

The survivors, shocked out of their sleep, set about the work of desperate rescue. One wounded man, with both legs blown off above the knee said, "I'm all right, get the badly wounded boys out." Another Digger had a mangled arm, but would not let his mates light his cigarette. "I'll have to learn to do it with one hand," he said, "and I may as well begin now."

While peaceful penetration dominated the Australian front, conventional fighting continued with small-scale, local operations. On May 19, the 6th Brigade attacked to clear Germans from the town of Ville-sur-Ancre, north of Morlancourt and to secure high ground south of the town. The 22nd Battalion was to capture this ground while the 21st, 23rd and 24th Battalions took the village itself. The plan called for an advance on a front of 1,200 metres and penetration to the same depth.

The 22nd's specific objective was to capture two sunken roads, codenamed Big Caterpillar and Little Caterpillar. Both were strongly defended by outposts and machine-guns. The Australian barrage fell at 2 am and the attackers, well spaced with around 15 metres between men, were through the outposts before the Germans could organise an effective resistance. But the defenders in Big Caterpillar were ready. Laying down sheets of rifle and machine-gun fire, they hammered the 22nd so hard that in one company all the officers were hit, leaving Sergeant William Ruthven to take command.

As his leading wave came under machine-gun fire from close range, Ruthven ran forward and threw a grenade, which landed beside the post. He bayoneted one of the crew and captured the gun. Coming upon enemy emerging from a shelter, he wounded two and captured six. Reorganising his men, Ruthven established a command post from which he noticed movement in Big Caterpillar. Armed only with a revolver, he ran across open ground and shot two Germans who refused to come out of their dugouts. Single-handed, he mopped up this post and captured the entire garrison of 32.

For the rest of that summer's day, Ruthven did all that was required of an acting company

commander; he moved about under fire to supervise the defence and to encourage the men and inspired everybody by his fighting spirit. It was a superb example of initiative, and it was rewarded with the Victoria Cross.

Little Caterpillar was a deep obstacle, but few Germans stayed to endure the artillery fire. Some even abandoned their machine-guns. However, in Ville-sur-Ancre itself the fighting was savage. The 23rd Battalion was engaged in a house-to-house struggle, during which the Germans twice fired at Australians after making signs of surrender. The Diggers were furious, especially since the victims of this perfidy included Corporal W.J. Flinn, one of the battalion's most popular men.

But there was more to come. Lieutenant J.A. Wiltshire of the 23rd, Lieutenant E.H. Edgerton of the 24th, and Lieutenant A.E. Reilly of the 21st, with their platoons, were involved in a spirited fight against Germans in good defensive positions behind walls. Again prisoners who had surrendered fired at Australians, whose indignation now centred on a German officer. In a fortified house, men of the 23rd Battalion tore him away from those of the 24th, who tried to protect him, and shoved him through a door into the street, where he fell. "Don't shoot him, he's mine!" Wiltshire shouted to the Australians there. Whereupon he hauled the terrified German to his feet, showed him Corporal Flinn's body and then shot him dead. Such grim episodes were not infrequent.

At the same time, two young Australian reinforcements taking part in their first battle had entered a house from which the Germans had been ejected. For the newcomers the battle appeared to be over, and having found a piano in the house they leaned their rifles against a wall and indulged in an uproarious sing-song. Their singing came to an abrupt stop as a floor trapdoor lifted in front of them and a German sergeant major, still armed, led out 10 men, also armed. The sergeant major surrendered to the astounded singers who had to reach hastily for their rifles to accept their unexpected captives.

The attack on Ville-sur-Ancre was a complete triumph and the casualties of 418 were not regarded as high, considering that at least 800 Germans were killed, while another 330 and 45 machine-guns were captured. And it went on like that with raid after raid producing success after success.

The day of May 31, 1918, went down as a momentous one in the proud history of the AIF. That was the day the Australian Corps was placed under Australian command for the first time. The new GOC was the redoubtable Lieutenant General John Monash, in succession to Birdwood, who himself was promoted to command the Fifth Army, superseding General Gough. Field Marshal Haig had long been impressed with Monash's abilities. He had a reputation throughout the British forces as a painstaking, methodical organiser who missed nothing, but at the same time he could simplify complex problems.

Some officers regarded Major General Brudenell White as the finest Australian commander, but, despite his brilliant record from Gallipoli onwards, he was junior to Monash in appointment. In any case, Birdwood took White with him as Fifth Army Chief of General Staff, while Monash appointed Brigadier General T.A. Blamey as his Chief of Corps Staff.

At the same time, the last two British divisional commanders in the Australian Corps, Generals N.B. Walker and N.M. Smyth, were transferred back to the British Army. Major General T.W. Glasgow took over the 1st Division, Major General Charles Rosenthal the 2nd Division, and Major General John Gellibrand succeeded to command of Monash's old division, the 3rd. Only one sour note marred the change-over to Australian command of the AIF. Birdwood was given the post of "administrative commander" of the AIF. It was a last attempt by the British High Command to retain a degree of control over Australian decisions and appointments. Birdwood had the good sense to suggest rather than order, and he did not interfere with Monash's plans.

An RE8 two-seater aircraft used by No. 3 Squadron, Australian Flying Corps, is fitted with incendiary bombs for a night raid. The Squadron's main role was reconnaissance, aerial photography and fighting-off enemy scout planes.

ACES HIGH

In January 1916 the British War Office made a special request to the Australian Government. It wanted 200 volunteers from the AIF to be trained and commissioned as pilots in the Royal Flying Corps. "Exceptionally good work has been done in the RFC by Australian-born officers, and the Australian temperament is specially suited to the flying service," the British note stated. The Australian military leaders approved the request.

The most successful Australian pilot in British service was Robert Alexander Little from Windsor, Victoria. Commissioned into the Royal Naval Air Service late in January 1916, he later became a captain and the 8th top-scoring British ace with 47 enemy fighters shot down. An ace was a flier with five or more victories. Little was awarded the Distinguished Service Order twice and the Distinguished Service Cross twice. He was 22 when shot down and killed on May 27, 1918, while attacking a German bomber.

The Australian Flying Corps had only four operational squadrons and one of these, No. 1 Squadron, spent most of the war in the Middle East. It produced the only Australian air Victoria Cross winner of the war, Lieutenant F.H. McNamara, who, when wounded himself, rescued a fellow flyer in Palestine.

Numbers 2, 3 and 4 Squadrons AFC, each with 18 planes, flew with the Royal Flying Corps and used many types of aircraft including the famous Camel, Sopwith Pup, Spad, Bristol Scout, Bristol Bomber and RE8. No. 3 Squadron was the first AFC unit to deploy in France, arriving at Savy on September 10, 1917. It was at once allotted to the newly formed Australian Corps as "corps squadron". In this role it scouted for the Australian divisions, fought strafing and bombing enemy aircraft, and flew close-observation or contact patrols during the AIF's 1918 battles. The squadron's RE8 aircraft established an astonishing record of service. Flying from 10 different aerodromes, they logged 10,000 hours of war flying, fired 500,000 rounds of machine-gun ammunition at enemy targets, dropped 6,000 bombs, and accounted for 57 enemy aircraft. Numbers 2 and 4 Squadrons served in an infantry support role with the 80th Wing RFC, which became the Royal Air Force in April 1918.

The leading AFC ace was Captain A.H. Cobby, DSO, DFC and two bars, of No. 4 Squadron, who shot down 29 enemy planes and 13 observation balloons. The other two leading AFC aces, also from No. 4 Squadron, were Captain E.J.K. McCloughry (23 victories) and Captain R. King, DSO, DFC, with 22.5 victories. All flew the Camel. No fewer than 57 Australian pilots became aces.

Commander of the RFC in France, General Sir John Salmond, reported in 1918: "The Australians showed the most remarkable aptitude for flying and air-fighting. Their squadrons were of wonderful quality and achievement. One in particular was perhaps the finest squadron that ever took the air."

He was speaking of No. 3, but all the AFC squadrons were composed of courageous and colourful men who risked their lives in their flimsy machines every moment they were in the air. Several of them were former Anzacs and many had fought in trenches in France. Thus they always knew, and appreciated, that their primary task was to help the embattled infantry below.

Right: A pilot's point of view from the cockpit of a Sopwith Camel of No. 4 Squadron. Dubbed the "Camel" for its hump-shaped cowling under the twin fixed machine-guns, this single-seater fighter plane was highly manoeuvrable and had a ceiling of 19,000 feet even when fully loaded with four 25-pound bombs. It was however a tricky aircraft for novice pilots, killing many on their first flight. Below: An AFC squadron sets out from a French airfield. The Australian pilots earned a dare-devil reputation, accounting for 435 enemy planes during the war.

Above: Ace pilot, Captain E.J. McCloughry (hands crossed centre) stands proudly with fellow pilots of No. 4 Squadron. This fighter squadron boasted top-scoring ace A.H. Cobby and a total score of 199 planes downed. Below: Soldiers examine an RE8 crash-landed on Westhoek Ridge due to engine failure.

The Australian Corps' first action under Monash took place on the night of June 10, when the 7th Brigade, led by Brigadier General E.A. Wisdom, was to capture a new German front-line defence system at Morlancourt and Sailly Laurette. Even for Australians, the 7th Brigade's morale was remarkably high, and some men who would not normally have taken part in the fight went to extreme lengths in attempts to be included. A private of the 25th Battalion, on duty as an orderly at a military baths behind the lines, left his post to go to the front. A corporal, away at a school of instruction, went absent without leave, but he arrived too late for the fighting. A Queensland officer, in hospital recovering from a head wound, crept out of the hospital and persuaded a friendly pilot to fly him to Morlancourt, but he, too, arrived after the fighting had ended.

Possibly the most remarkable officer in action that day was Captain M.G. Hammond, whose left arm had been paralysed by a wound received at Flers in November 1916 and which he carried permanently in a sling. Though unfit for active service, he was so persuasive that he had taken part in the fighting at Broodseinde in 1917. And he remained so soldierly that his men of the 28th Battalion were happy to have him lead them. He had risen from the ranks, he had been decorated with the Military Medal and the Military Cross, and his courage commanded respect. At Morlancourt, he hooked a walking stick over his paralysed arm and held a watch in his right hand so that he could follow the operation timetable.

From experience at Passchendaele, Hammond knew that the impetuous Australians often pressed too close to their creeping barrage. Now, ordering his company not to get in front of him, he walked at a carefully measured distance behind the bursting Australian shells. Often he turned his back to the enemy and straightened out his own line of men with a wave of his stick. When he held the stick above his head the men, as ordered, lay down. Hammond himself remained standing. He studied his watch, and when it was time for the advance to continue, he twirled his stick as a signal. While visiting his posts the next day, Hammond was seriously wounded and was carried out of the action. "Keep the old flag flying, sir," he said to his CO, Lieutenant Colonel P. Currie, as the bearers took him past battalion HQ. Aged 26, he died of his wounds a few days later. Some of his tough soldiers wept when they heard, and hundreds visited his grave. "By God, he died game," one of them said, echoing the feelings of all.

The Australian success was complete. At a cost of 400 casualties, they captured all the German defences at Morlancourt, inflicted heavy casualties and took 325 prisoners, 30 machine-guns and six trench mortars.

Still separated from the rest of the Australian Corps, the 1st Division kept up its relentless campaign of peaceful penetration throughout May and June, but sometimes its units also carried out larger operations. One of these was an attack on Merris, in the Lys Valley, by the 10th Battalion under Lieutenant Colonel M. Wilder-Neligan, famed throughout the AIF for his leadership during two years of fighting. In what was officially termed a "minor operation", a platoon led by Lieutenant J.M. McInerney had reached its first objective and was digging in when a machine-gun concealed behind a hedge fired on them at close range.

McInerney and a number of others were killed and the situation of the survivors became desperate. Corporal Phillip Davey rose up and attacked the gun with grenades and put half the crew out of action. Having used all available bombs, he returned to the original jumping-off trench, grabbed another supply and ran back to the attack. The Germans had reinforced the machine-gun post, but Davey killed all eight crew and captured the gun. He then dragged the weapon into his own new post and repelled infantry counter-attacks supported by artillery. Davey was seriously wounded about midday, but his actions had been so decisive that when the fighting ended at 1.30 pm, all objectives were in Australian hands and Merris was surrounded. For high courage and fortitude

In an idyllic picnic setting at Corbie, Australian, English and American troops lunch together on July 3, 1918, the day prior to the Hamel battle. Respectful of the Diggers' experience, the Americans trained under Australian units.

Davey won the VC. He was a tough soldier. He had been accidentally wounded in March 1917, and gassed in October that year. In January 1918 he had won the Military Medal for bravery during a night partol. His wounds at Merris put him out of the war at last.

Monash had inherited the fight for Ville-sur-Ancre. The plan had been Birdwood's not his own. Since then, Monash had advanced north of the Somme River at Morlancourt and he was eager to make a similar advance south of the river. This led him to plan his first big battle as Australian Corps commander. The obvious target was Hamel, a strongly fortified village north east of Villers-Bretonneux and a key defensive post for the Germans. The new British Mark V tanks had arrived in France and the Tank Corps commander, Brigadier General Hugh Elles, wanted to redeem the reputation of armour in Australian eyes. He was keenly aware that since Bullecourt, more than a year before, the Australians had placed no trust in tanks. He invited Monash and Blamey to inspect the new models in exercise. The Mark V which Elles showed the Australians was the first British heavy tank which one man could drive by himself and the first to be powered by a specially designed tank engine. Two other virtues distinguished it. It had a rear turret for the commander, and Hotchkiss machine-guns in place of the Lewis guns. These guns required only a relatively small aperture for the barrel, thus allowing the ball-mounting to swing across a greater arc of fire.

Monash and Blamey were duly impressed and saw the possibility of using the tanks to reduce infantry casualties. This was a paramount consideration because recruiting in Australia had declined alarmingly and influenza was further reducing the AIF ranks. Overall, the five Divisions were short 8,255 men, about 10 per cent below optimum strength.

Monash could allot only 7,500 men to the capture of Hamel and he proposed to use four brigades, one from each of the 2nd, 3rd, 4th and 5th Divisions. In this way, all divisions would gain experience from working with tanks and no one division would have to bear all the losses. The force would be commanded by Major General Sinclair-MacLagan of the 4th Division. Because American troops had been training under the Australians, Monash asked for 2,000 Americans, organised in eight companies. Also, he wanted one or two tank battalions — 36 or 72 tanks. He was given 60.

In a markedly successful public relations exercise, the Tank Corps invited Australians of all ranks to inspect the tanks. With native curiosity, the Diggers climbed all over them, inside and out, and were taken for rides across the training fields. Some Diggers even persuaded the British crews to allow them to drive the monsters. Meanwhile, Australian infantry and British tank officers discussed infantry-tank tactics. The new tanks moved almost as fast as running infantry, and could be manoeuvred rapidly. Even before battle, the Diggers came to like them and each company gave a name to the tank allotted to it, such as Eureka, Gloria and Aussie.

The Australians had, from their first meeting, also liked the American soldiers, and they were pleased to be going into battle together. The Americans, or Doughboys, as they called themselves, were distributed among the Australian battalions by platoons so that they came under experienced Australian leadership at a low level of rank. The Australians' only criticism of the Americans was that they were a bit too effusive and emotional. American officers made speeches and the Diggers were always embarrassed by speeches.

A few hours before the battle was to begin, an American major climbed onto a tree stump to address his men, and his words were recorded by an Australian correspondent, F.M. Cutlack. "I just want to tell you boys that you are going into a good keen fight among the Australians and you're going to give the Huns hell," the American major declared. "The Australian authorities say they want all the papers captured on the enemy for information purposes — remember that. If I find any man has looted papers he has no right to keep, he's in for trouble. Now you're going into action with some mighty celebrated troops guaranteed to win, and you've got to get up to their level and stay there with them. There'll be a whole heap of people looking on at you, and you've got to make good."

The Germans had learned nothing of the imminent attack. The noise of the tanks' approach was screened by artillery fire and by bombs dropped from aircraft. At some points, the tanks were late for the start time of 3.10 am and the infantry had to go on without them. But their general performance was impressive. The Diggers approached behind the tanks, which were marked with the infantry's own battalion colours. The tanks tore gaps in the wire and shed machine-gun bullets as if they were mere hailstones. Their greater speed than earlier tanks took them lurching across enemy trenches rather than into them and their machine-gunners provided steady covering fire for the following infantry.

For the first time, ammunition was dropped to Australian troops by parachute, the idea of Captain L.J. Wackett of 3rd Squadron, Australian Flying Corps. Dropped from bomb racks at an altitude of 1,000 feet, each canister carried one box of ammunition — 1,200 rounds — and each plane averaged four trips. In all, 93 boxes were dropped, saving the infantrymen an immense amount of hard and dangerous work.

Some Australians, keyed to battle pitch by previous experience and equally by General Monash's meticulously detailed combat plans, found the battle itself something of an anticlimax. Private F.W. Roberts of the 21st Battalion wrote at the time: "Left support trench at 1.30 am loaded like a mule. Usual fighting order — 220 rounds, two Mills bombs, extra water bottle, shovel down the back and a pannier for the Lewis gun — all hellish weighty. Knees knocked when barrage opened but after

At 4th Brigade headquarters in a quarry south of Hamel, officers are briefed on Monash's battle plan for taking Hamel. General Haig praised Monash as a commander "who thinks out every detail and leaves nothing to chance."

the start all trepidation vanished. Wonderful barrage put up, ground shrapnel shell on explosion lit up the scene and we caught glimpses of Fritz going for his life. No return barrage and no machine-gun fire. An easy walk over. Slung my gun and stumbled across. Experiencing none of the 'blood lust'. A most prosaic affair. Met no Fritzes myself until neared final objective. Spared his life to rat him but found nothing." Other Australians were more successful in their searching of captured Germans' pockets and belongings and finished the battle laden with souvenirs.

The precise Monash had allowed 90 minutes for the battle to be won. It took 93. The capture of Hamel and the accompanying diversionary attack at Ville-sur-Ancre were dramatic successes. Vaire and Hamel Woods fell to the 4th Brigade, while the 11th, with its tanks, quickly mastered Hamel village. The Australians held the whole of Hamel Valley and were on the eastern or forward slope of the last ridge, from which the Germans had been able to overlook country held by the Allies.

Perhaps 2,000 Germans were killed or wounded, and 1,500 were taken prisoner. Also captured were two field guns, 32 trench mortars, two anti-tank machine-guns and another 177 machine-guns. Only three British tanks were disabled, and they were recovered. The total casualties of the attacking infantry were about 1,400. The Americans, in their first Western Front battle, had performed "bloody well", according to their Australian mates. They suffered 176 of the killed and wounded

Hamel was a comparatively minor action in terms of the length of front and numbers of men engaged, but Field Marshal Haig himself acknowledged that the battle strengthened the British position and weakened the Germans at Villers-Bretonneux.

The main value of Hamel was as a model for

A casualty of the Hamel operation, a Mark V tank lies crippled outside the village where a victorious tricolour flag flutters from the rooftops. Only three of the 60 tanks engaged in the battle were knocked out.

almost every attack afterwards made by British infantry with tanks. Hamel was a lesson in how to use the Mark V tank with aggressive infantry in breaking through German trench lines. While the Tank Corps commanders and General Monash were responsible for the overall plan, the specific tactics were developed during the course of the battle by the enterprising Australian troops and the enthusiastic British tank crews. They learned, for example, that it was not necessary for the infantry to stay immediately behind the tanks for protection; they could fan out into line on either side of a tank and from here their view forward was not obscured. Another example of cooperation tactics was that the infantry leader with a tank could stop it and ask the commander to concentrate on a particularly stubborn enemy post, perhaps by crushing it.

One of the important phases of every battle was the mopping up afterwards, but it became more essential when working with tanks because now there were not successive waves of infantry to do the job. Mopping up was a euphemism for the killing or disarming of all enemy found hiding in the labyrinths of trenches, dugouts, galleries, passages and ruined buildings which made up the German defensive system. The risk of being shot at from the rear by Germans left alive or not firmly taken prisoner was great, and many enthusiastic but inexperienced Americans were killed in this way. The Australian infantry understood the importance of mopping up and carried it out with ruthless efficiency. Sometimes, while an attack swept on, a few Australians had to be left behind to lay siege to deep dugouts until their occupants surrendered, usually encouraged by Mills grenades and phosphorus bombs.

The Hamel success came while the Supreme War Council was meeting at Versailles and its members were lamenting that, apart from the Australians' peaceful penetration program, there seemed to be little progress against the Germans. There had been no offensive operation by any of the Allies since the previous autumn and the Hamel victory was electrifying.

The French President of the Allied War Committee, Georges Clemenceau, visited the headquarters of the 4th Division near Corbie, Somme. He said that he had come specially to speak to the men who had fought at Hamel and a large number of them grouped informally around him. He spoke in English: ''When the Australians came to France the French people expected a great deal of you. We knew that you would fight a real fight, but we did not know that from the beginning you would astonish the whole continent. I shall go back tomorrow and say to my countrymen 'I have seen the Australians. I have looked in their faces. I know that these men will fight alongside us again until the cause for which we are all fighting is safe'''.

Hamel marked the end, once and for all, of the mainly defensive attitude of the British front, and it forced Field Marshal Haig and the senior commanders to examine the possibilities of offensive action on similar lines by similar means. Monash wanted to organise another and larger offensive at once. When this was denied he gave orders, on the afternoon of Hamel, that all Australian divisions in the line were to return to ''vigorous offensive patrolling''. His soldiers were only too pleased to obey. In broad daylight on July 6, Corporal Walter Brown of the 20th Battalion, from his forward observation post, stalked a German officer and 11 men and terrorised them into surrender by threatening to throw a grenade at them. He won the VC for his daring act.

Captured German documents covering the period June 25 to July 13 and circulated by General Headquarters to all commands were, in effect, testimonials to the Australian infantry and its leadership. Those issued by the German Second Army Headquarters, under General Von der Marwitz, bemoaned: ''In the case of the present trench division, it has often happened that complete piquets have disappeared from the forward zone without a trace.''

There was more than a hint of desperation in an announcement made in a written order of the day by the CO of the 43rd Reserve Division in the Hamel area and found on a German taken prisoner. It stated: ''I will give three weeks' leave to the first man who brings in a prisoner or equipment enabling us to identify the regiment holding the opposite sector.''

It was said that the German report which most pleased General Monash was one dated July 13: ''During the last few days the Australians have succeeded in penetrating, or taking prisoner, single posts or piquets. They have gradually — sometimes even in daylight — succeeded in getting possession of the greater part of the forward zone of an entire division.''

Such praise from the enemy whetted Monash's appetite for more decisive battles. And he was soon to satisfy his desire.

HEROES WITHOUT GUNS

A stretcher-party of seven men struggles back with a wounded comrade through a muddy morass on Passchendaele Ridge in August 1917.

"Don't forget me, cobber"

Having given first aid, stretcher-bearers gently lift a casualty of Third Ypres onto a stretcher for conveyance to the nearest aid post. After a battle subsided, stretcher-parties from both sides would negotiate a brief, informal truce to collect their wounded.

STRETCHER-BEARERS

Fighting soldiers often said that stretcher-bearers working in the open during battle were the real heroes of the war. Unarmed and necessarily upright when carrying, they constantly risked being hit by bullets and pieces of shell. The Red Cross armband they wore was often no protection, and many bearers were hit by deliberate sniper fire.

The AIF field ambulances had bearers, all members of the Australian Army Medical Corps. In addition, the infantry battalions had their own bearers, most of whom were members of the band when out of action. Thousands of Australians volunteered to become stretcher-bearers to bring in wounded mates, despite the days of devoted, arduous and harrowing work it often took to clear the wounded from a battlefield after heavy fighting. The labour was so exhausting that in heavy mud a team of eight bearers was needed to get a wounded man to a regimental aid post or field ambulance. Still, many bearers collapsed during the treacherous kilometre-and-a-half carry from the front line to the aid posts.

Lieutenant Simon Fraser of the 58th Battalion wrote of the stretcher-bearer's work after an action at Fromelles where his company had brought in more than 250 wounded: "It was no light work getting in with a heavy weight on your back, especially if he had a broken leg or arm. One foggy morning we could hear someone calling for a stretcher-bearer; it was an appeal no man could stand against so some of us rushed out and had a hunt. We found a fine haul of wounded and brought them in. I came across a splendid specimen of humanity trying to wriggle into a trench with a big wound in his thigh. Another man about 30 yards out sang out, 'Don't forget me, cobber.' I went in and got four volunteers and we got both men to safety."

Throughout the battles on the Western Front, the shout most frequently heard above the shattering noise became "Stretcher-bearer!" Due to their devotion, those calls rarely went unanswered; if a wounded soldier went unattended it was because all available bearers were already busy or because they too had joined the frightening toll of casualties.

A lightly wounded but unconscious soldier is carried to safety. Suspicion by both sides that fatigue parties were using Red Cross flags and armbands for cover often led to the sniping of genuine stretcher-bearers.

Right: Delivered safely to a Regimental Aid Post behind the lines, a soldier is fitted with a splint for his fractured leg. Aid posts contained beds for patients unable to travel further by ambulance. Below: Under escort, German prisoners bring in Australian wounded. Using enemy prisoners as stretcher-bearers discouraged German snipers, who were unwilling to fire on their own men.

Top: At an advanced dressing station in Ypres, a soldier stares blankly into the distance — a classic symptom of "shell shock". Driven mad by barrages, men ran suicidally from their trenches, or collapsed, screaming gibberish, even calling for their mothers. Many never fully recovered composure of mind. Above: Stretchers are unloaded from a trolley on a light railway track from the front line. The journey was more comfortable than by hand-carrying; rail trolleys and horse-drawn sledges also traversed thick mud more easily.

tagged for his "ambulance" ride — four stretchers stacked in a converted army truck — to the nearest military hospital.

5

EAST OF AMIENS

With all five AIF divisions side by side, the next Allied assault aimed at driving the enemy away from Amiens. After years of tense trench warfare, the fighting now took place in open fields as wave upon wave of Australian and British soldiers delivered a shattering blow to the German Army.

A hazard of luring Germans from their bunkers is illustrated in Dyson's sketch "Looking for Booby Traps".

While the Australians were still basking in their successes at Hamel and Merris, the German High Command had been planning a major attack against the French. This time, Field Marshal Ludendorff chose as his objective the great defensive bastion of Rheims, west of Verdun. The intention was to break through at Chateau Thierry, west of Rheims, and towards Chalons, east of Rheims. This would effectively isolate the strategically important and psychologically significant city.

French Intelligence on this occasion was better than usual and the Allied Supreme Commander-in-Chief, Marshal Foch, anticipated the German blow, which fell on July 14. He had carefully laid plans for a counter-offensive, and within an hour of the German attack, he ordered his own to begin on July 18. To lead this response he chose General Charles Mangin, one of France's best fighting generals.

Mangin was also impressed with Lieutenant General Monash's model battle at Hamel earlier in the month, though his own attack was to be on a much greater scale. Foch had given him 13 French divisions, plus four American divisions equivalent in manpower to eight French divisions. All told, he had 200,000 men to lead at the enemy. The spearhead formation was the formidable Moroccan Division, recently in action with the Australians at Villers-Bretonneux. The infantry was backed by 2,100 guns and 325 French tanks. Mangin's objective was the recapture of the city of Soissons, north of Chateau Thierry, and his troops attacked with such spirit that by nightfall they were within five kilometres of the city. The Germans were alarmed.

When the French counter-blow fell, Ludendorff was in Flanders supervising the positioning of troops and guns for another attack on the British lines. As reports reached him from the south, he at once ordered the newly arrived units back to the Soissons sector. In fact, a second danger was looming for the Germans. Foch had wanted a double thrust and initially this was to be made by the British in the Lys Valley, the sector favoured by Field Marshal Haig. Foch, however, preferred the offensive to be made along the line of the Somme River, and Rawlinson and Monash supported him.

One excellent reason was that much of the river valley was suitable for tanks. Another was that the AIF's punishing tactics had so badly shaken the Germans that they had not adequately strengthened their positions. Intelligence reports showed that German troops feared to be sent out to erect wire defences and build strong points opposite the Australians. In constant dread of attack, the working parties achieved little.

Keeping up such pressure was exhausting to the Australians and they hoped for a rest. They were sure they were going to get it when they heard that the Canadians were coming south from the Arras front to relieve them. But the Canadians' movement was connected with the big new attack being planned and the Australians did not get their rest. Their morale remained high, nonetheless, largely because of Monash's concern with their welfare. He stressed to his officers that their men's well-being was their first duty, and he insisted on good food and plenty of recreation.

Monash also did his best for the recruiting drive in Australia with a cable which he sent on July 13: "Since the opening of the German offensive in March every division of the Australian Army in France has been engaged and always with decisive success. Those who are privileged to lead in battle such splendid men are animated with a pride and admiration which is tempered only by concern at their waning numbers. Already some battalions which have made historic tradition have ceased to exist as fighting units and others must follow unless the Australian nation stands by us and sees to it that our ranks are kept filled. Nothing matters now but to see this job through to the end, and we appeal to every man to come, and come quickly, to help in our work and to share in our glorious endeavour."

The British attack along the Somme was entrusted to General Rawlinson and his Fourth Army, of which the Australian Corps formed part. While Monash did not plan the overall attack, the methods employed were based on those he had used at Hamel. Moreover, the meticulous details of planning owed much to Monash's example. The attack was based on the use of 430 British tanks, which would lead the three stages of the advance. To achieve maximum surprise, no preliminary bombardment was intended and low-flying aircraft would drown the noise of the assembling tanks. The infantry — Australians, British and Canadians — would be close behind the tanks, and all three divisions of British cavalry were to exploit the anticipated infantry breakthrough. The date was fixed for August 8.

The AIF 1st Division in the Hazebrouck-Merris-Strazeele area at last received orders to move south to the Somme sector. This would bring all five Australian divisions together under Monash — highly desirable militarily, but a matter of some distress to the Belgian folk who had come to depend on the Australians for certain economic arrangements. One of the 1st's battalions had been in billets at Vieux

Berquin near Hazebrouck, and when it was about to move the usual torrent of claims from villagers flooded in. The claims officer demurred over one demand for 300 francs for four ducks, a petticoat and a pair of knickers. He accepted the ducks, but baulked at the petticoat and knickers. "If one of my men has a petticoat and knickers," he told the lady claimant, "then some girl gave them to him as a souvenir."

"Ah no, you don't understand," the lady said. "They were taken from my clothes line to carry away the ducks." The officer saw the logic of this and approved the claim.

Meanwhile, as troop strength built up around the Somme, the ever ready Australian raiders continued to keep the Germans off balance. On the night of July 29, units of the 5th Division's 8th and 14th Brigades captured yet another system of German defences at Morlancourt, the scene of so many Australian exploits. The raiding parties seized two trench lines each 100 metres long and captured 138 Germans, 36 machine-guns and other weapons. The infuriated Germans brought up a fresh Württemberg division and hit back in strength, but by this time the Australians had been relieved by troops of the British III Corps. Thus, the Württembergers missed the hated Australians and instead captured 282 British troops along with the trenches. British HQ was alarmed because some of these men had valuable tactical information. However, the Germans learned nothing about the impending British offensive. The Australians were annoyed by the incident. Once again, they said, gains they had made at some cost had been given away by the British.

Monash had in the meantime planned a new and special use for Australian Flying Corps aircrews. Delays in receiving battle information had always worried him. Without rapid transmission of information, his staff was unable to give the infantry the support it urgently needed, such as covering artillery fire or more ammunition. More importantly, there was always the very real risk that if information was more than an hour old when it reached HQ it could be dangerous; a company reporting that it needed help from the artillery might then move forward and be caught in bursting shells from friendly guns. Monash proposed to overcome the problems by using the 3rd Squadron of the Australian Flying Corps on what he termed contact patrols.

Flying at no more than 500 feet, two-seater planes carrying pilot and observer would constantly study the progress of battle. The observer would mark on a map the precise movements of Australian infantry, enemy positions and other vital facts, then the pilot would fly at top speed to drop the map, in a weighted multi-coloured streamer, to a waiting soldier-cyclist. Monash expected to have the necessary information within 10 minutes of its origination over the front.

As the build-up continued, the incoming Canadians were well hidden and none were to be put into the front lines until the night of the assault. If the German High Command were to learn that Australians and Canadians both were assembling on the same stretch of front, they would greatly strengthen their defences. Two elite forces at the one place could only mean a major attack.

Despite the intense security, rumours spread within the AIF that a great new offensive was imminent. The Australians reckoned that with their man Monash playing a key role, it had a good chance of success. When planning reached the stage of decision about which men would be taking part and which would be left out, some of those omitted asked to be paraded before their company commander to request the "right to fight". Their officers patiently explained what the men already knew; that each unit needed an experienced cadre on which to rebuild should casualties be heavy.

The day before the attack, an incident occurred that spoke volumes about the calibre of the Australian fighting man. In a small wood near the Bois l'Abbe, on the left of Villers-Bretonneux, 13 British carrier tanks, loaded with ammunition, bombs and petrol, were concealed in readiness for the assault. With

Private J. Himes, known as "the souvenir king", sits possessively amid his collection of German mementos picked up at Polygon Wood. Scrounging was a favourite AIF pastime, often undertaken out of necessity to supplement poor supplies.

time on their hands, the tank crews invited a crowd of gunners from Australian artillery brigades in the area to look over the tanks. The Tommies gave many of the curious Diggers some instruction about steering and control, which was a lucky thing as it turned out.

The Germans had been lobbing over nuisance artillery from time to time, and later in the day one random shell hit a tank. The explosion hurled up a cloud of bursting ammunition, burning petrol and tree branches, and German gunnery observers, thinking that they had hit a dump, ordered a concentrated bombardment. As shells thundered into the wood, the tank drivers ran for cover.

The Australian gunners, not themselves under attack, quickly tired of watching and about 20 Diggers rushed in to try to save the tanks. The intense bombardment was tossing trees about like twigs and earth was erupting in fountains. The gunners vanished into the smoke, dust and flame and everyone watching thought that they had committed suicide. But, surprisingly, after a few minutes one of the tanks came slewing and clanking through to safety, followed by four more, all with novice Digger drivers at the controls.

The camouflage on one tank caught alight. The Australian inside stopped the vehicle in the midst of the barrage, hopped out and ripped off the camouflage, then clambered inside again to continue his rescue. An English officer, overcome with emotion, threw his arms around the neck of an Australian major. "Those chaps aren't men," he said. "They're bloody archangels!" One of his archangels, Gunner J.S. Bannon, was mortally wounded while attempting to put out a fire in another tank.

Late that afternoon, before the Australians began a night march to their jump-off position, a message from their Corps commander, John Monash, was read to them: "For the first time in

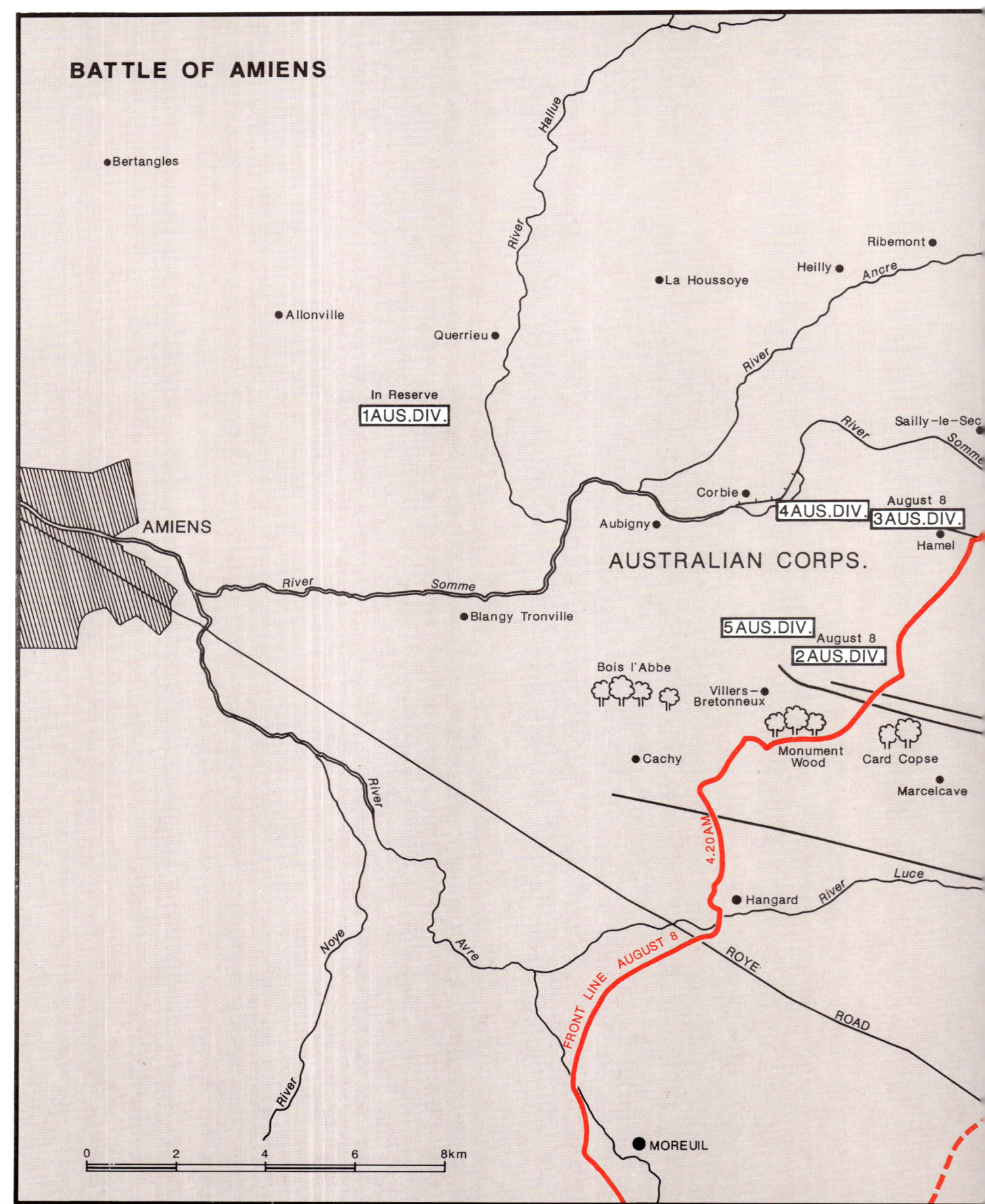

All five Australian divisions were together on the Somme for a big push against the enemy away from Amiens and Villers-Bretonneux. After a series of

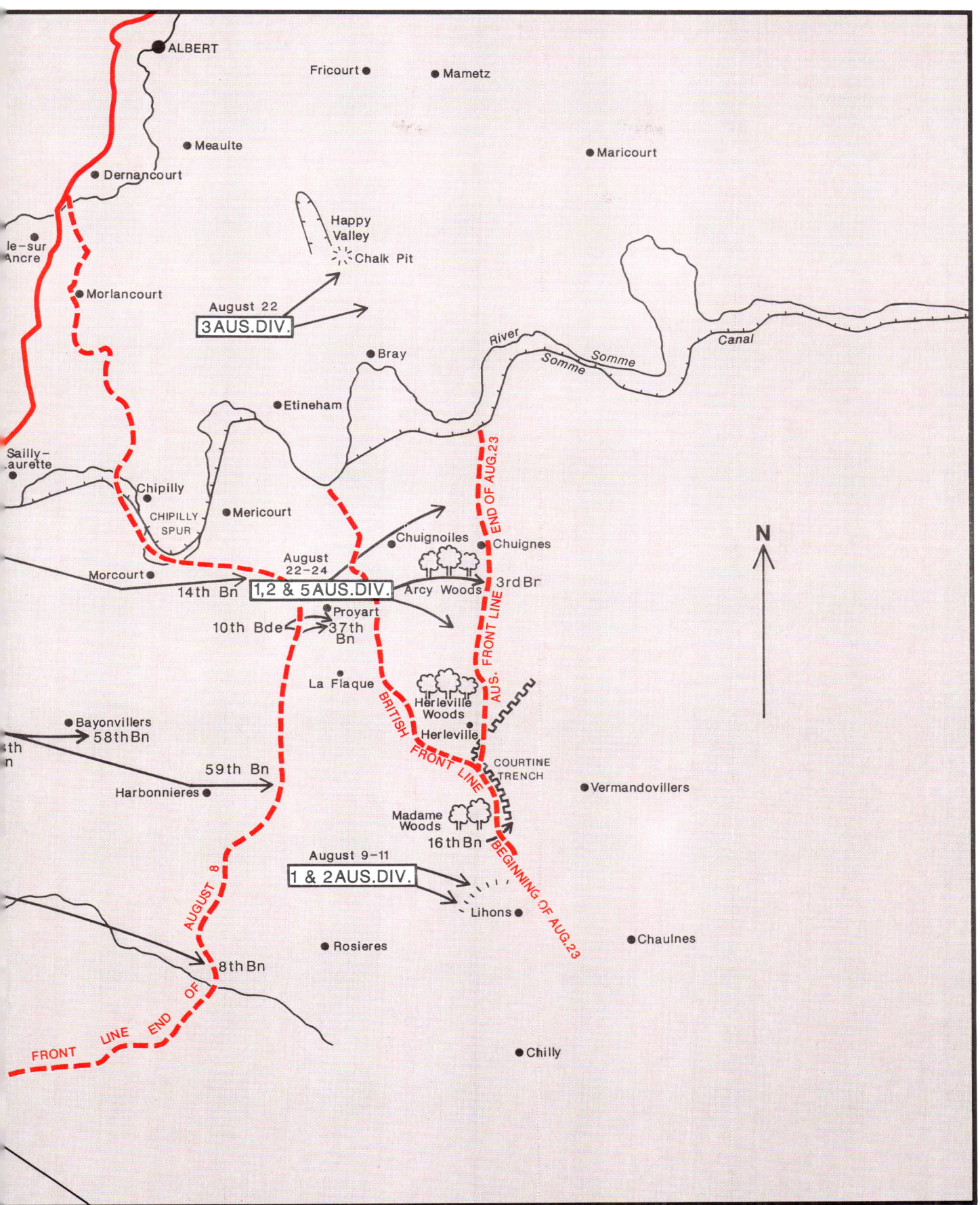

decisive Allied victories, the Germans retreated east of Chuignes while the AIF reorganised to stage yet another assault.

the history of this Corps all five divisions will tomorrow engage in the largest and most important battle operation ever undertaken by the Corps. They will be supported by an exceptionally powerful artillery, and by tanks and aeroplanes on a scale never previously attempted. The full resources of our sister Dominion, the Canadian Corps, will also operate on our right, while two British divisions will guard our left flank.

"Because of the completeness of our plans and dispositions, of the magnitude of the operations, of the number of troops employed, and of the depth to which we intend to overrun the enemy's positions, this battle will be one of the most memorable of the whole war; and there can be no doubt that, by capturing our objectives, we shall inflict blows upon the enemy which will make him stagger, and will bring the end appreciably nearer.

"I earnestly wish every soldier of the Corps the best of good fortune and a glorious and decisive victory, the story of which will re-echo throughout the world and will live forever in the history of the home land."

What would be known as the "Battle of Amiens" was to begin at 4.20 am on August 8. Dense fog had fallen over the Somme but most of the 100,000 assault troops found their way to the start line along 20 kilometres of front. Each of the two AIF divisions immediately involved, the 2nd and 3rd, had a front of 3,600 metres. In close support were the 4th and 5th divisions, ready to leapfrog the 2nd and 3rd at the point and time specified in Monash's plan.

The men of each battalion moved to their tape line and lay down, wet and cold but full of anticipation. Some of the guiding teams were apprehensive about losing their way but none did. The 57th aimed for lights specially set up by its scout officer; they were candles in old petrol tins with holes to form the numerals 57.

Two brigades of the 2nd Division and two of the 3rd were to begin the attack and their leading men crawled forward to within 80 metres of the enemy trenches. Behind them other infantry, pioneers, engineers and Stokes-mortar crews were loaded and ready to go. Rumbling up from behind came the tanks, ready to take the lead when the British, Canadian and Australian guns opened up.

Without the usual bombardment, the Germans were taken completely by surprise and by 7.30 am the offensive had broken the Germans' line so thoroughly that much of their field artillery was overrun and captured. This stroke ensured fewer casualties among the advancing troops.

For the first time in the war, the support troops kept pace behind the assaulting wave, instantly ready to continue the advance when the leading troops had captured their objectives. While the men of the 2nd and 3rd divisions dug in, those of the 4th and 5th leapfrogged and at 8.20 am took up the second, open phase of the advance. The infantry formation now changed from extended line with men spread out left and right, to sections of 10 men in single file. Over the entire battlefield, many hundreds of sections wormed their way forward in company with tanks and gun teams. Close behind, came supply wagons.

After years of struggle in the trenches the war on the Western Front had reached the stage of field fighting. When the second wave of four AIF brigades swept on into open warfare without a break in momentum, the Germans were astounded. Staff officers in positions of supposed safety found themselves looking down the barrels of .303 rifles and rear gun-battery crews were swallowed up while loading shells into the breeches of their guns.

On the ridge south of Morcourt, the 14th Battalion was held up by machine-guns. Following a message dropped by an AFC contact patrol, a section of the 39th Battery of the AIF Field Artillery came up at the gallop and under intense fire knocked out the enemy guns at the close range of 730 metres.

In Morcourt itself, the 14th Battalion, with tanks to help, captured hundreds of German reserve troops and seized masses of stores. Despite this unexpected but welcome distraction, the unit quickly reorganised and

BLIGHTY

The Australian soldiers' presence in England during the war began as a love affair, but the relationship slowly turned sour. When the first Anzacs arrived in London in 1916 they were hailed by the British press as heroes, and warmly welcomed by individual Britons. The Australians, most on their first visit to the old country, were genuinely excited to see the distant land known from childhood history lessons and text books as "Home".

Affectionately known as Blighty, England was the wartime haven for AIF soldiers on leave or for those badly wounded enough to be admitted to an English hospital for treatment and rest. (The slang term "blighty" described their wounds.)

Having collected pay and a new uniform from the AIF Headquarters in Horseferry Road, the Digger on leave was free to explore London's tourist spots, have a "good feed" at a hotel, and to go to the theatre. There was also a chance of an invitation to tea with society ladies or lunch and a stay in the country at a manor house. But as the war continued, the cordial mood in England changed.

In London, however, prostitution grew enormously and began to take its toll on the visiting soldiers. The rate of venereal disease in the Australian Army to June 1917 reached an alarming 14.4 per cent; many Diggers left England angered because of it. But the troops did not have a mortgage on war-ravaged emotions. Many British lasses were left brokenhearted by unfaithful Australians.

Disillusionment grew on both sides. Empire loyalty was eroded so much by the slaughter in France that by 1917 the Diggers sang a new version of the song "Dear Old Blighty". It went: "Blighty is a failure, take me back to Australia". Drunkeness and petty theft, initially treated with lenience, were less tolerated after riots at AIF camps in 1918. Some shops and hotels began to refuse the Australians service and accommodation. The Diggers in Blighty soon learned of the temperamental and cultural gap between the two Allied nations. One homesick writer lamented: "I hardly realised what a great country Australia is until I left it".

A hoarding above London's YMCA headquarters welcomes Australia's Diggers. Despite efforts to save the lonely soldier from temptation, the nearby Strand was notorious for prostitutes.

A postcard sent from England boasts of the Diggers' popularity with the young ladies of London.

At a cottage in Weymouth convalescent camp, soldiers exchange money. Many were shocked that Australian currency was not accepted in England.

The civilised pleasures of Blighty made it across the English Channel to Paris, where British and Australian officers on leave enjoy a singalong in a sumptuous recreational club. The club offered reading rooms with English books and newspapers.

Above: Having collected pay and information on London accommodation from the AIF Administrative Headquarters, and picked up a clean uniform from the Clothing Store, soldiers congregate outside the War Chest Club to plan sightseeing. *Below:* Instantly recognisable to curious British passersby, slouch-hatted Diggers meet at Trafalgar Square fountain where lonely soldiers looked for their mates or hoped to attract the attention of a friendly English girl.

"What do you think of London, mate?" asks an officer in Cecil Hartt's cartoon. "There ain't a blessed verandah-post in it," was the Digger's nostalgic reply.

Lieutenant R. Davies addresses his weary and depleted platoon from the 29th Battalion before the Battle of Amiens. With thick fog and heavy smoke blanketing the countryside, it was vital for the men to stick close together.

joined in the third stage of the advance. This stage was to have been carried out by infantry brought forward in Mark V Star tanks, mammoth vehicles with seating for 20 infantry. Oversized and underpowered, and with their crews exhausted, they ground to a halt, but the infantry went on without them and captured the intended positions, just short of the old Somme battlefields of 1916.

In one of the most dramatic episodes of an eventful day, sixteen Rolls-Royce armoured cars now raced ahead of the infantry and caused panic and havoc among the Germans. Fanning out onto side-roads, they fired into German headquarters, billets and messes, and so demoralised the Germans that many units became incapable of facing the more dangerous threat posed by advancing Australian infantry. The 58th Battalion captured Bayonvillers without a fight and the 59th, having succeeded in driving the Germans out of Harbonnieres, ran the Australian flag up on the church tower at 11 o'clock.

A lively action developed at Card Copse, towards which the 28th Battalion had advanced from Villers-Bretonneux. The Germans had purposely left a single gap in their barbed wire defences in hopes that the Australians would funnel through it and be slaughtered by machine-guns sited opposite. The 28th fell into the trap and was stopped cold. Lieutenant Alfred Gaby, a 24-year-old company commander, rushed the German position. Running along the parapet, oblivious to the murderous fire, he emptied his .45 revolver into the garrison, drove the crews from their guns and forced the surrender of 50 Germans with four machine-guns. Rapidly reorganising his men, he led them on to his company's final objective, which he captured and held. Gaby was living dangerously, but had much yet to do.

The Germans held Chipilly Spur, a long, hairbrush-shaped ridge which protruded across and commanded the Somme valley. It was a strong defensive position and Monash and his staff feared that its garrison would inflict heavy

An armoured car and scouts of the 15th Brigade probe ahead of the main infantry advance between Bayonvillers and Harbonnieres on August 8. Rolls-Royce cars became a swift and deadly weapon in the ensuing battle.

casualties on the advancing British and Australians. During the morning, two NCOs of the 1st Battalion, Company Quarter Master Sergeant J.C. Hayes and Sergeant H.D. Andrews, crossed the river to search Chipilly village for souvenirs. On their return they suggested that they should take a reconnaissance patrol to the spur itself, but at the time the 2/10th London Battalion was about to attack so the idea was turned down.

Shortly thereafter, an AFC contact patrol reported that the British division to which the 2/10th belonged had stalled three kilometres back. At 5.30 pm, worried about lack of progress, Brigadier General Iven Mackay of the 1st Brigade ordered a patrol sent out. Hayes and Andrews were at once chosen, and with four men were ordered to pinpoint the trouble and help the division forward.

Crossing the river at 6 pm, Hayes sought out a company commander of the Londons, Captain J.S. Berrell, who warned him that it was too dangerous to go on. Nevertheless, Hayes spread out his few men and made a successful rush under fire. Dividing into two parties, the six Australians searched the village and spotted all the German positions from the rear and flank. Andrews, with one man, scouted nearly one-and-a-half kilometres ahead of friendly troops. Meanwhile, encouraged by the Australians' boldness, some of the Londoners came forward.

In a succession of quick and decisive little actions, Hayes and Andrews took several enemy positions, capturing Germans and machine-guns and handing them over to the Londoners. As the remaining Germans retired from Chipilly ridge, eastwards across the Somme River, Andrews fired at them with a German machine-gun. The enterprise was over by 10 pm and, having led the British advance the entire way, the Australians prepared to return to their company.

Before they departed, Hayes took the precaution of asking Captain Berrell for a note, in which the British officer commented on the Australians' "conspicuous work and magnif-

LITERALLY LOUSY

Lice were the great scourge of the trenches and the constant and inevitable companion of every soldier. The tiny insects flourished in the seams of dirty clothing where their eggs were incubated by body heat. They caused frenzied scratching.

Widely known as "chats" among Australians, lice were pale fawn in colour and left blotchy red marks all over the body except on the head; they also created a distinctive sour, stale smell. Captured German dugouts had a species of small red lice crawling over the walls and blankets.

In spare moments the Australians launched major offensives on their shirts and underclothes, either running their fingernails or a lighted candle along the seams. Each division had its own baths where, if lucky, the men would go once a week. About 10 or 12 at a time, they splashed around for 15 minutes in hot soapy water while their tunics and trousers were put through a Foden Disinfector or delousing machine. Soiled underwear was piled in lorries and sent back to the Corps laundry.

A fair proportion of the eggs remained in the clothes and within a few hours of being put on a man's body heat hatched them out. Lice transmitted an infectious disease known as trench fever. A common preliminary symptom was acute shooting pains in the shins followed by high fever. Treatment called for between six and 12 weeks off duty. The disease was a continual and heavy drain on manpower and accounted for 15 per cent of all cases of sickness in all the British armies.

Nits infested the men's hair and every company had a barber to shave them to the skull. Many Australians objected to this and tried to keep a reasonable amount of hair.

Soldiers search clothing for lice ("chats"). The stock joke reply to civilians who asked about life in the trenches was: "We just sit around chatting."

Rats, another of the trench vermin, become a starving French soldier's only meal.

icent bravery with me today". It was a wise move. The official records of the 2/10th London Battalion did not mention the six Australians, yet they had silenced all enemy machine-guns on Chipilly Spur, cleared the village itself and 2,000 metres of ground, captured about 300 prisoners and brought the English front in line with their own. It was an astounding performance for which Hayes and Andrews were each recognised with the Distinguished Conduct Medal.

By the end of the first day, the British attack had gathered in 13,000 prisoners and more than 200 guns. The French, in a supporting operation, took another 3,500 prisoners. Not surprisingly, Ludendorff wrote that August 8 was "the black day of the German Army". A hole 20 kilometres wide and 11 kilometres deep had been punched into the German defences and only characteristic German resilience and tremendous effort prevented a greater breakthrough. Men and guns were rushed from all parts of the front to plug the gap.

The AIF 1st Division had arrived on the battlefield from the north on August 8, but the very next day, with the 2nd Division, it took over the Australian lead and captured the Lihon heights. North of the Somme River, the British III Corps was making little progress and Monash was ordered to assume command of that sector as well. He formed a composite division, known as Liaison Force, of the 13th AIF Brigade and the 131st American Regiment, which had been attached to his corps. Moving eastwards as a column across open country, Liaison Force, under Brigadier General E.A. Wisdom, captured the villages of Bray and then Etineham from the panicking Germans. Another column, which pushed forward south of the Somme River, was not so quickly successful and fought for two days to capture vital ground above the village of Proyart.

But then the situation began to deteriorate. Coordination between senior British, Canadian and Australian commanders fell off after the second day of battle, August 9. The generals were so busy congratulating one another on their amazing success that they did not devote enough attention to the business at hand. Progress was uneven and some units were left dangerously exposed on their flanks.

As a result of this lack of coordination, the Australian infantry had to rely on its own initiative. Under the prevailing conditions even the most brilliant troops could not avoid heavy loss of men. The 1st Division, so successful at such low cost in Flanders, lost 100 officers and 1,500 men in three days during the August advance. Killed on August 11 was Lieutenant Albert Gaby, who again led his company of the 28th with great dash to its objective. The Germans responded with heavy machine-gun and rifle fire and everything depended on the Australians digging in quickly. Gaby walked along his line of posts, encouraging and directing his men, and while thus engaged he was shot dead by a sniper. Gaby was awarded the Victoria Cross.

On the day Gaby was killed, many great commanders assembled at the Red Chateau in Villers-Bretonneux to discuss the victory and consider further advances. Field Marshal Haig was there with his Chief of General Staff Lieutenant General H.A. Lawrence, the Fourth Army commander, General Rawlinson, and General Sir Henry Wilson, Chief of the Imperial General Staff. Georges Clemenceau turned up unannounced and joined the talk. Others present included the Canadians' leader, Lieutenant General Currie, and, of course, Lieutenant General John Monash. They spread maps on the grass under a great beech tree and assessed the degree of the German defeat. The consensus was that the Germans were on the run and with this in mind most of the commanders present at the beech-tree meeting believed that only a general push was necessary to drive the invaders from the French and Belgian soil.

It was not to be as easy as that; it never was with the Germans. Their resistance was stiffening by the hour and the Canadian commander, General A.W. Currie, operating on

German dead litter captured trenches towards Lihons after 11th and 12th Battalion troops had attacked on August 10.

Monash's right, told him that fighting by methods of open warfare was daily growing more costly. In fact, the enemy had recovered from his first surprise, many British tanks had been knocked out by artillery fire and much British heavy artillery had not yet had time to come up. Cheap exploitation of the success of August 8 had come to an end.

A few kilometres to the east of Villers-Bretonneux the AIF 10th Brigade knew that the fighting was far from over. Heavily engaged for some days, it was advancing on Proyart village where the Germans were making a desperate stand. The 40th Battalion was required to cross 1,200 metres of open ground swept by machine-gun fire from high ground to the east of the village. It was acting in collaboration with the 37th Battalion, which was held up by several machine-guns. Sergeant Percy Statton of the 40th could see the line of guns preventing the 37th's advance and he turned his Lewis guns on them while a sergeant and 10 men of the 37th made a gallant rush at the machine-gun position. All were shot down.

At that, Statton, armed only with a revolver, took three men and led a dash across 750 metres of open ground. The German gunners, intent on the 37th Battalion, did not spot Statton and his party until too late. At the first gun, the sergeant shot two of the crew while his mates killed another three. Racing to the second gun, Statton shot the whole crew except one, for whom he had no bullet remaining. The surviving German lunged at Statton with his rifle and bayonet. Side-stepping, the Australian wrenched the rifle from his enemy and bayoneted him. As the Australians headed for the next two guns their crews fled, only to be wiped out by the Lewis

The 13th Australian Light Horse sets out to join the 9th Brigade's assault near Bray on August 22. The horsemen, however, were not employed after Britis

gunners whom Statton had sited earlier.

During the action one of Statton's men was killed and another badly wounded. When the 37th's advance continued, Statton again went out, this time to bring in his dead and wounded mates. He was to receive the VC for his valour.

On the same day that Statton was adding to the laurels of the AIF, its commander, John Monash, was reaping his own reward. He was summoned to Bertangles, the site of Haig's HQ, where King George V conferred on him a knighthood. To witness this event, 500 Australian soldiers who had fought in the recent battle — 100 from each of the AIF divisions — had been brought to Bertangles. Captured guns and other trophies of war were hauled in from the battlefield to provide an appropriate background for the ceremony. The King was interested in the German transport horses and remarked to Monash, "I hope that they will soon learn the Australian language." Monash, with a different and more colourful form of Australian language in mind, murmured that he had no doubt that the horses would pick it up.

According to Captain C.R. Duke, in a letter home, August 8 and 9 were "easily the best two days the Australians have ever had in France and it did 'em more good than six weeks in a rest area. I wouldn't have missed it for anything and only hope that they give us another show like it every three months. Our chaps are as happy as Larry and singing at the top of their voices."

But as always, the rollicking song of victory had its dark choruses. In the week of August 7-14, the five Australian divisions suffered 6,491 casualties, 20 per cent of their strength upon entering the battle.

Yet the AIF had the satisfaction of knowing

avalry proved too vulnerable to German machine-gun fire.

British and Dominion troops advance eastward in late August as the powerful combination of Mark V tanks and infantry, now together in open country, put pressure on German defences on the Somme.

that it had achieved all its objectives and that it had inflicted greater losses, taking prisoners into account, than the enemy. Their total loss was 12,000 according to German records. Equally significant, at Rosieres and La Flaque the Australians captured huge dumps of engineering materials which provided the AIF with all its needs for the rest of the war. There were two complete railway trains, horses, wagons, lorries and tractors by the hundred, as well as field searchlights, mobile pharmacies, motor ambulances, field kitchens, gun limbers and ammunition carts. In addition, they had taken vast quantities of ammunition — so much the less to be fired at the British forces.

After August 14, the Australian divisions, on which the next advance depended, had to be reorganised and given some rest, so for a week the attack was suspended. The advance was resumed early on August 22, with the 9th Brigade, 3rd Division, on the right wing. The Brigade attacked with its 33rd and 35th Battalions side by side between Bray and Happy Valley. South of Bray, the 3rd Pioneer Battalion made crossings over the Somme River.

The attack went well and everything seemed ready for the next phase when, at 5.30 pm, the Germans counter-attacked the British 47th Division, on the left flank of the 9th Brigade. As the British were forced back, the 33rd Battalion was left hanging grimly clinging to a chalk pit beyond the mouth of Happy Valley. The 9th Brigade's reserve battalion, the 34th, pushed out a northern flank to protect the 33rd and the brigade held on all that night and next day in an apparently impossible position until relieved by the 10th Brigade.

During the fighting on August 23 there occurred one of the most audacious individual exploits of the AIF on the Western Front. No less an observer than C.E.W. Bean regarded it as second only to Albert Jacka's feat at Pozieres two years earlier.

Close to Madame Wood, just west of

Vermandovillers, two Australian battalions, the 16th and 13th, and one British battalion, the 16th Lancashire Fusiliers, were to advance across a kilometre of open ground criss-crossed by scores of enemy trenches, and drive the Germans from a defence system known as Courtine Trench. The 16th took its objectives without much difficulty, but the Lancashire Fusiliers did not link up as planned. Lieutenant Lawrence McCarthy, commanding D Company of the 16th, personally led a platoon and bombed his way along Courtine Trench. He found that the Lancashire men had failed to take their objectives.

The situation was critical. In the trench the Germans had built an earth block between themselves and the Australians and were defending it with machine-guns. One was firing along the trenches won by the Australians. McCarthy set two British soldiers, members of a liaison party from the Lancashire Fusiliers, to dig through the earth block. With Sergeant F.J. Robbins, he scrambled up and around the block and into the trench beyond. He shot a sentry at another barrier and rounded a bend to find a machine-gun firing over his head back at the Australians. Shooting the gunners, McCarthy raced on and came up behind a German officer giving orders to his men. McCarthy shot the officer and the men bolted into a short trench on the right. McCarthy and Robbins threw Mills bombs at them. Just then, the two Fusiliers, having dug through the block, arrived with a Lewis gun and prevented German reinforcements from joining the fight.

At this point, a German waved a blood-stained handkerchief from the right trench and 40 enemy filed out to surrender. Another 15 lay dead in the trench. The shaken survivors closed in on McCarthy from all sides, wrenched from his hand the revolver with which he was attacking them and patted him on the back in their intense relief at still being alive. In 20 minutes of furious action, McCarthy had killed 20 Germans, captured 50 more and seized five machine-guns. He handed over to the Lancashire Fusiliers more than 700 metres of trench which they had been assigned to capture in the first place. His VC citation noted that he had "saved a critical situation, prevented many casualties and was mainly, if not entirely, responsible for the final objective being taken." The men of his battalion regarded his action as "a super VC stunt".

Meanwhile, the 1st Division, on a front of six-and-a-half kilometres, fought in jumbled valleys and ridges to capture positions between the Somme Canal on the left and Herleville Wood on the right, with the town of Chuignes as their objective. The 2nd and 5th Divisions relieved the 1st on August 26 and the Germans continued to wilt under the pressure. Given a rare opportunity to perform in open country, the 13th Light Horse did valuable work on the Australian front and flanks. On their horses, they could quickly carry out a reconnaissance and provide harassing fire from a spot unexpected by the enemy.

Following a bayonet charge by the 3rd Battalion, which cleared Arcy Wood, near Chuignes, the AIF captured its greatest trophy, a 15-inch naval gun. The gun, with its carriage, platform and concrete foundations, weighed more than 500 tonnes. With a barrel 21 metres long, it fired a shell weighing a tonne more than 38 kilometres. For months, its crew had systematically bombarded Amiens. Within minutes of having captured the gun, Australian soldiers were sliding into its barrel to pose for photographs. Monash was no less proprietorial than his men. Claiming the right to dispose of the giant gun, he proposed to present it to the city of Amiens.

But the string of easy victories was too good to last. On the evening of August 29, enemy opposition began to stiffen around Clery, three kilometres north west of the city of Peronne. Early the next morning the 3rd Division launched yet another attack on the enemy lines. It was the beginning of the great fight known to Australian military history as the Battle of Mont St. Quentin.

DIGGER

In a cartoon sketched on a farmhouse door, a 2nd Division Digger defiantly taunts the Kaiser — to the delight of soldiers billeted at Beaucourt. Known for their graffiti and ironic signposts, Digger humorists also contributed jokes and cartoons to AIF newspapers.

"They put laughter into everything"

AN ORIGINAL CHARACTER

From early 1916, Australian soldiers, some of whom had been miners in civilian life, had been heard calling themselves "Diggers". The term, however, was not entirely new; it had already been in common use among New Zealanders. After the battles of Bullecourt the name of "Digger" started to spread among Australian soldiers. They readily accepted it because it described their most frequent activity, especially in the trench lines.

"Digger" became a term of respect among AIF men and by the end of 1917 soldiers of other Allied armies were using the same greeting when speaking to Australians.

Apart from their contrived name and easy language, the Australians were also known for their informality, which was often confused with a lack of formal military discipline. Coming from a country with a thin military tradition, the Diggers were not prone to conform easily to convention. This was certainly so in the men's casual attitude towards their higher ranks; the Diggers often did not salute them, especially British officers. The irreverent Australians were also renowned as a race of jokers and humorists. Phillip Harris, editor of the Diggers' own newspaper, *Aussie,* said of them: "They put laughter into everything."

Rough and ready on the one hand, revelling in sport, gambling and, where possible, womanising, the Diggers also had an unashamedly soft side as well. They were helpful to civilians in need, and they had an especially sentimental streak when it came to children and animals. Above all, it was their uncompromising originality that often stood out in the fiercely unmoving mood of the battle front. In a letter home, an 11th Battalion sergeant, J.M. Aitken, summed up the classic Australian character: "He is a fighter, a born fighter; each Australian has his separate individuality and his priceless initiative which made him better than the clockwork soldier."

A wounded American soldier is helped from the battlefield by two Australians. The spirit of Digger mateship embraced their Yankee comrades. After their first action together at Hamel in July 1918, an Australian officer reported, "United States troops are now classified as Diggers."

Saviours of Amiens, two Australian soldiers help grateful citizens of the town return home with their few worldly possessions.

Displaying an unabashed sentimental streak, cooks of 27th Battalion play with their pets, nicknamed "The Royal Family".

Resting his pack's weight on his rifle, a Digger takes a "smoko" break. British poet John Masefield admired the utilitarian Australian uniform and hat, which were not "idiotic clothes designed for the parade ground".

An all-male cast rehearse for an open-air concert party at Villers-Bretonneux. Some AIF concert party groups, like the "Coo-ees" and "Whizbangs", became renowned performance troupes with musical and comedy repertoires.

Competitors and spectators at the 9th Brigade swimming carnival in May 1918 enjoy inter-battalion races and the chance to cool off at Rivery, near

"Come in spinner!" cries the coin-tosser in a two-up game at an Australian camp behind the lines. The tedium of camp life was relieved by gambling, organised sports and self-devised entertainment.

Amiens. Football matches, boxing tournaments and horse races also stimulated camp life for sportsmen and gamblers alike.

In the cheerful firelight glow of a billet in Ypres, a Digger spins a yarn for his captivated audience. The staunch light-heartedness of the Digger, cocky

nd high-spirited, was as remarkable as his ferocity in battle and selfless devotion in mateship.

6
THE CLIMAX AND THE COST

Wanting an exclusively Australian victory, Monash risked his weary men to force the enemy back to the Hindenburg Line. The Diggers stormed the fortress of Mont St. Quentin and, despite dwindling forces, broke the back of Germany's defence, ending the war in a blaze of glory.

Having considered the results of the fighting between August 8 and August 21, Field Marshal Haig urged a new approach to operations. "To turn the present situation to account," he told his officers in a general order on August 22, "the most resolute offensive is everywhere desirable. Risks which a month ago would have been criminal to incur ought now to be incurred as a duty. It is no longer necessary to advance in regular lines and step by step. On the contrary, each division should be given a distant objective which must be reached independently of its neighbour, and even if one's flank is exposed for the time being. Reinforcements must be directed to points where our troops are gaining ground, not where they are checked. The situation is most favourable. Let each one of us act energetically and without hesitation push forward to our objective."

Having spent the entire war reinforcing failure, Haig was now urging his commanders to reinforce success, a basic military dictum. However, he modified his instructions to Rawlinson. His Fourth Army could be rather more relaxed than the other British armies. It

Dyson captures the spirit of mutual dependence and support that characterises Digger mateship in his compassionate "Walking Wounded".

had attracted the German reserves to its front and could hold them there. There was no immediate need to push the Germans from the battle-torn ground in the great bend of the Somme near Peronne.

Monash, however, had contrary ideas. His troops had been fighting for 18 days and tank support was no longer available, but Monash considered the Australian Corps to be invincible. Haig's general policy of aggressiveness suited him admirably and he read it as an order to be continually at the Germans' throats. He directed the 2nd and 5th Divisions to maintain pressure and move ahead by infiltration, but to avoid frontal attacks that might cause heavy losses. Major General John Gellibrand had hoped that his exhausted 3rd Division might be relieved, yet Monash ordered him to press forward north of the Somme River and keep abreast of the others. If all went well the doughty 3rd would get a good rest later. In Monash's view, the 4th and 1st Divisions were the ones in need of immediate relief. On August 24, the 4th Division was replaced at Lihons by a French division and went into reserve. The 1st Division followed it on August 26, having suffered 70 officer casualties and 1,354 others since August 23.

Monash had a great ambition. He wanted what he called an "exclusively Australian achievement". Under Haig's guidelines, he considered himself justified in making plans without consulting Rawlinson, his direct chief, though Rawlinson would have to consent to them. The AIF battalions were below strength and only a few reinforcements were arriving. Moreover, there was a serious lack both of tanks and heavy artillery. The battered condition of the roads and the heavy congestion on them prevented many of the heavy guns from coming up. But Monash had limitless faith in his tough veterans and he was willing to bet everything on them. Haig had ordered that risks were a matter of duty; Monash meant to do his duty.

His strategic object was to render the line of the Somme River useless to the Germans as a defensive position and thereby hasten their retreat to the Hindenburg Line. The tactic by which he hoped to achieve this was an attack on the key position of the whole line, the dominating hill of Mont St. Quentin. Lying a kilometre-and-a-half north of the river town of Peronne, the hill guarded its northern and western approaches. The hill was barely a hundred metres high, but the Germans regarded it as impregnable. The whole operation, Monash told his staff, must be mounted without delay; the Germans should not be allowed a single extra hour to establish themselves ever more strongly on the hill.

On August 27, Monash explained to his divisional commanders that, in pursuing the Germans, each attacking brigade had to be "kept in line until it has reached the limit of its endurance." The order caused a certain amount of resentment because the troops were so tired from physical strain and lack of sleep that they could be seen by the roadside, fast asleep. Even the sturdiest of sergeants was staggering with fatigue. Nevertheless, the order was accepted and the men prepared to obey it.

Monash held a conference at the 2nd Division's HQ on the afternoon of August 28; another at 3rd Division HQ on the 29th and a third at 5th Division's HQ later that same day. At these meetings Monash allotted to each division an immediate and ultimate objective: the 5th Division was to take the Peronne bridges, then a wooded spur east of Peronne; 2nd Division was to aim for the bridgehead at Halle, then Mont St. Quentin; and 3rd Division was directed towards high ground north east of Clery, then Bouchavesnes spur.

Monash put his audaciously direct and meticulously detailed plans to Rawlinson on the afternoon of August 30. Mont St. Quentin itself, he said, would be taken by three battalions in the direct part of the assault.

Having listened attentively, Rawlinson remarked, "So you think you are going to take Mont St. Quentin with three battalions! What presumption! However, I don't think I ought to stop you. Go ahead and try. I wish you luck."

Monash had gone to Rawlinson out of

formality, not to seek advice. Even before he visited Rawlinson, he had ordered Major General Charles Rosenthal, commanding the 2nd Division, to send his reserve brigade, the 5th, under Brigadier General E.F. Martin, across the river at Feuilleres. It was to secure a bridgehead on the Clery side of the river, opposite the Somme bend at Ommiecourt. The 5th found Clery partly occupied by Germans and the trench systems east of it strongly held. After some skilful manoeuvring, the Brigade reached its objectives and, with slight casualties, captured 120 prisoners and seven machine-guns. The bridge at Ommiecourt was damaged but reparable for an infantry crossing. Monash was now ready for his great Australians-only battle.

Marshal Ludendorff and the German General Staff were no less aware than Monash of the importance of Mont St. Quentin. Ludendorff predicted that an attack would result in disaster for the British, and to make certain he sent the 2nd Prussian Guards Division to hold the hill "to the death". Among the units of this renowned division were the Kaiserin Augusta and Kaiser Alexander Regiments, as much celebrated in Prussian tradition as the Coldstream and Grenadier Guards in Britain.

To form a strong garrison for nearby Peronne, the German High Command took the unusual step of calling for volunteers. The ramparts were manned by men drawn from many experienced units, and scores of machine-guns were sited in positions from which they could sweep the approaches. The river flats lying in the angle of the Somme between Clery, Mount St. Quentin and Peronne were a mass of barbed-wire defences. Cover for any attacking force was scant and the few ruins which dotted the landscape were manned as strong points by the Germans.

Major General Rosenthal detailed his 5th Brigade to open the attack. In its weakened state, the total strength of the assaulting infantry was only 70 officers and 1,250 other ranks. This was scarcely one third of a brigade's normal strength, and it seemed a pathetically small force to conquer a fortress. Indeed the companies of the 34th Battalion had dwindled from four platoons to three and the platoons to about 15 men, instead of more than 30. They were strong in Lewis-gun teams, but the gun teams comprised only two or three men, who carried half a dozen magazines instead of the usual six men with 15 or 20 magazines.

Rosenthal's 2nd Division battalions to assault Mont St. Quentin were the 17th, 18th, 19th and 20th, all from NSW. One or another would be the reserve at various times. Because of their weakness and the enemy's strength, and the amount of open ground to be covered, the task was one of the most formidable ever faced by the AIF. The standard strength of a company was supposed to be 120 men; the 17th and 18th averaged 70, the 20th had 60 and the 19th only 50. It was not possible to get a hot meal to the men on the night of August 30, but at 3 am next morning a carrying party arrived with an issue of rum. Somebody in the rear had sensibly decided that in view of the men's weariness on a chilly night, the old AIF rule of keeping the rum until after action could be broken.

The Australian barrage fell at 5 am. Five brigades of field artillery, 150 guns, concentrated their fire on a 2,300-metre arc, low on the mount, with a gun to every 23 metres of the first line and half that in the two later stages. The rate of fire was two rounds per gun per minute. Four brigades of heavy 8-inch guns which had arrived at the last minute — about 90 of them — dropped their shells on the back areas, summit and flanks.

On the right, the 17th started along the Clery-Peronne road. The Australians encountered enemy posts at once and, charging with a yell, demoralised the Germans, most of whom surrendered. Their captors pointed to the rear where wounded Australians still able to walk took them in charge. Without the manpower to collect captured machine-guns, the advancing Diggers had to leave them behind.

Incredibly, along the whole face of the mount, the Germans ran back, heading for its more defensible northern and southern shoulders.

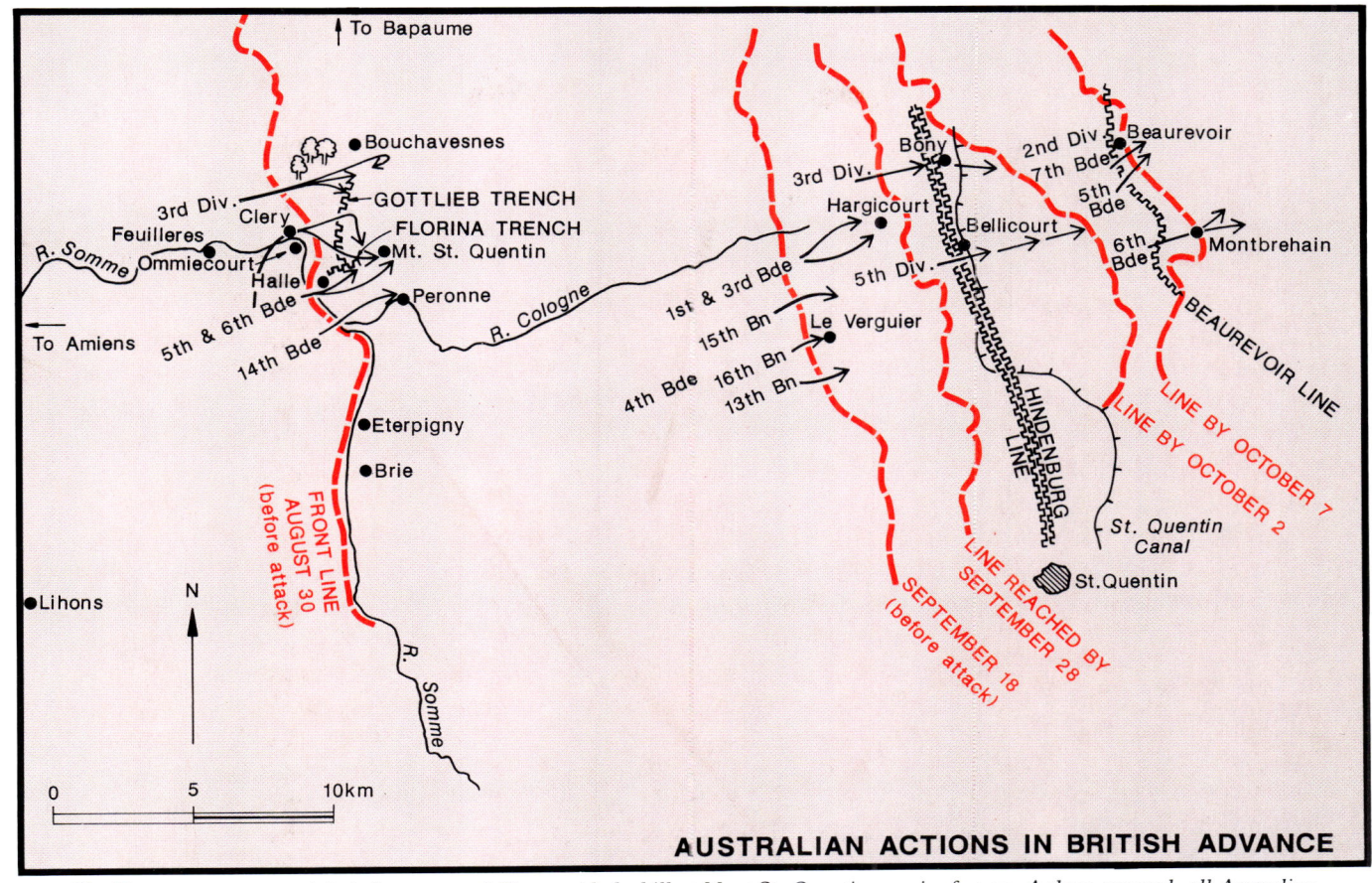

The Germans concentrated their forces around Clery, with the hill at Mont St. Quentin a major fortress. A three-pronged, all-Australian assault forced the Germans back to the Hindenburg Line where the five AIF divisions, in their last battles, continued the onslaught.

Trotting to catch them, the Australian riflemen of the 17th and 20th Battalions stopped for occasional shots. Lewis gunners, whenever presented with a cluster of enemy, threw themselves down to fire accurately. Many Germans of the elite regiments garrisoning the mount ran themselves into a state of breathless exhaustion and fear, and could not speak when first captured.

The reason for the rout at this phase of the battle soon became clear. Since the Australians' success at Hamel, and increasingly since August 8, the AIF's reputation had preceded it into the German positions. The Germans had heard, and they believed, that the Australians were merciless with their bayonets. On top of that, having been convinced that Mont St. Quentin could never be captured, the rapid Australian attack had demoralised them. Monash's tactics, of flank attacks combined with a frontal assault, hastened the process.

Having reached the first major objective, Gottlieb Trench, the Diggers sat along the parados and relaxed over a smoke while the guns still pounded the top of the mount and beyond. One 20th battalion soldier, stretching himself out on the ground, said, "If Jerry had known how tired I am he'd have stayed and beaten me," and then he went to sleep.

A company of the 17th Battalion, working in small parties over the right front of 1,000 metres cleared Park Wood and Halle, where the houses and trees were comparatively intact and many enemy machine-guns were firing. Lieutenant H.T. Allan saw three companies make a bayonet charge far up the mount, and it was he who reported that the hill had been taken. The battalion commanders, back a little from the fighting line, already knew from the large numbers of prisoners passing through to the cages that the offensive was going well. Now they were jubilant.

At his HQ near Amiens, General Rawlinson was dressing for the day when Major General

Archibald Montgomery, his Chief-of-Staff, telephoned him. "The Australians have captured Mont St. Quentin," he said.

"Have they, by God!" Rawlinson said. "That's a magnificent performance." Later he called it "the finest feat of the war."

He passed on the news to Haig, who was astounded. He had regarded Monash's operation as little more than a diversion and a characteristically self-indulgent Australian one at that. He himself had intended to turn the German line on the Somme by a quite different thrust from Bapaume. With Monash's success he at once gave orders for the Australian Corps to be supported. The British commanders were even more astounded when they learned that the "impregnable" Mont St. Quentin had been captured by eight exhausted companies of infantry totalling 550 men, with a few score machine-gunners and four companies of 200 men in close support.

When Rawlinson and then Haig heard the news, the battle was not yet over. The famed Alexander and Augusta Regiments, however, were broken. Meanwhile the Australian battalions on the flanks came up against stubborn resistance. On the left, the 3rd Division had attacked Bouchavesnes spur, from which the Germans could dominate Mont St. Quentin. The leading battalion, the 33rd, under Lieutenant Colonel L.J. Morshead, was held up by machine-guns in the heavily garrisoned Road Wood. Despite a gap of 500 metres between his left flank and a supporting British unit, the

German pioneers construct a bridge over an enormous crater near St. Quentin on the Hindenburg Line while stretcher-bearers stream past. By late Septem

Australian line advanced but took heavy losses. The greatest danger occurred at 6.20 am when the battalion was held up by an enfilading machine-gun. Private George Cartwright, facing withering fire, stood up and moved forward, stopping every few steps to bring up his rifle and shoot. He killed three of the machine-gun team in this fashion, then rushed ahead and hurled a grenade at the post. As it exploded, he charged, capturing the gun and eight prisoners. Practically the entire battalion had watched this feat in awestruck silence. Now the men stood up, cheered and furiously pressed the attack to a successful conclusion. As his mates hoped and expected, Cartwright was honoured with the Victoria Cross.

Still the 33rd held only part of the objective and Monash was becoming anxious. At 8.35 am he displayed the ruthless streak which his staff knew he could exercise in an emergency. "Casualties no longer matter," he told Gellibrand over a field telephone. "We must get Bouchavesnes spur and protect Rosenthal's left." Gellibrand understood the urgency and pushed his commanders harder. The spur was secured and the Mont St. Quentin assault force was safe from a left flank attack.

On the far right of Monash's arc of attack, at Peronne, the 14th Brigade attacked powerful defences. Since August 8, it had been the 14th's fate always to be the reserve brigade of its division and every man in it felt aggrieved. Now, on September 1, it was in the thick of the fight, and after the 53rd Battalion overcame a 77 mm field gun causing casualties with close-range fire, the Brigade's advance continued.

To the British commanders far from Mont St. Quentin, its capture within hours might have seemed like a walkover. That it came as the result of hard fighting by determined, courageous infantry was attested by the award of no fewer than seven Victoria Crosses. The recipients were: Private William Currey of the 53rd Battalion; Private George Cartwright, 33rd Battalion; Sergeant David Lowerson, 21st Battalion; Private Robert Mactier, 23rd Battalion; Lieutenant Edgar Towner, 2nd Machine-Gun Battalion; Corporal Alexander Buckley, 54th Battalion; and Corporal Lawrence Weathers, 43rd Battalion.

Perhaps the most remarkable of the episodes concerned was that which led to the only posthumous award of the seven. It involved Private Robert Mactier and it occurred when his 23rd Battalion was attempting to move into position for the assault on Mont St. Quentin. Lieutenant F.J. Jenkins was leading the attack with his company from a position known as Florina Trench. Jenkins found that he could make a detour through another trench which would get him to his allotted position without a fight, but since time was short, he was forced to use the direct route. His company started out in single file from Florina Trench and crossed the

918 the Hindenburg Line was under bombardment.

A LUCKY GENERAL

John Monash emerged from the conflict of 1914-1918 as the most impressive general of the war. The son of Jewish parents who had emigrated from Prussian Poland to settle in Victoria, Monash was a scholar and gentleman rather than a "natural" soldier. A professional civil engineer, he had qualifications in law and a deep knowledge of archaeology and medicine. A brilliant pianist and competent artist, he spoke fluent German and reasonable French.

He had been a member of the Militia since the age of 19 and in 1908 he was appointed to command, as a lieutenant colonel, the Victorian section of the Australian Intelligence Corps, the forerunner of the Australian Army's General Staff. In 1913, in this spare-time army, he was made full colonel and given command of the 13th Brigade. A year later he was on his way to war.

Monash was nearly 50 when he first experienced battle as a brigade commander at Gallipoli. His work there was unremarkable, but he flowered as major general commanding the 3rd Division, which he trained in England and took to France. He won a high reputation for organisation and personal courage under General Sir Herbert Plumer at Messines and Third Ypres.

His reputation as a really great commander rests on his achievements during the last six months of the war, after he became commander of the Australian Corps. In all but name he was an army commander. Monash was known as a lucky general because his predecessor as AIF commander, General Sir William Birdwood, together with his splendid chief-of-staff, Major General Brudenell White, handed over to Monash the finest fighting force on the Western Front.

Monash created nothing new. His genius was that he knew how best to use the tools at hand. He used the machine-gun barrage and the smokescreen to perfection. Under Monash's orders, it took an Australian officer at the Battle of Hamel to show that supplies could be air-dropped to troops. Not having been involved in the bloodbaths at Bullecourt, Monash had not lost confidence in tanks. He understood how they and infantry should cooperate. He also realised the importance of sophisticated transport and communications, of armour and airpower, and of organisation allied to flexibility.

Monash's biographer, A.J. Smithers, considered that he was "the first 20th century general, a man with petrol in his veins and a computer in his head."

The capture of Mont St. Quentin and Peronne was his most dramatic victory, even though he flouted his own principles concerning preparation. His men were tired, he had no tanks or heavy artillery, and he had to get his troops from south to north across the Somme River. Depending on surprise and speed and pushing his men to the limit, he achieved both.

Monash's men had confidence in him because they knew he cared for them. He found time, when preparing detailed battle plans, to give orders about hot meals and drinking water reaching the front line. Out of action, the Diggers accepted that he would do all that he could to make their hard life tolerable. Even so, towards the end, pride in his soldiers caused him to ask too much of them.

As the war ended, Monash accepted the post of Director General of Repatriation and Demobilisation. With his usual sharpness of intellect and wholehearted commitment, he kept 180,000 Australians busy and reasonably happy, and got them all home within a year.

General Monash ended his military career with a personal tragedy. After he had left Melbourne for the war in 1914, his wife Victoria found that she had cancer but concealed this from her husband throughout the war and after. For five years she kept up a flow of letters which gave no hint of her condition. Lady Monash died two months after seeing her husband return home, honoured by the world as a great and victorious commander.

Major General Sir John Monash poses formally outside his divisional headquarters at Glisy.

The Australian victory in Peronne in September 1918 is celebrated by renaming a street in true Digger fashion.

Peronne Road, which cut the northern edge of Florina Trench. Resuming the advance along a trench, the company spearhead came across a German machine-gun behind a barbed-wire barricade. A little further on were two similar posts. Corporal R. Finlay, at the head of the company, led an attack, but was instantly killed and the assault bogged down.

Lieutenant Jenkins, from his command post, sent Private Mactier to investigate. Armed with a revolver and grenades, Mactier dashed forward through the leading Australians and right up to the barricade. Throwing a bomb, he climbed over the wire, killed the gun-crew and threw the weapon out of the trench. His mates advanced and saw Mactier capture the garrison of the second post. Without pausing, Mactier attacked and killed the occupants of a third machine-gun post.

To attack yet a fourth post, Mactier scrambled out of the trench and was approaching his target when another gun swung around and riddled him with bullets. His extraordinarily persistent courage enabled the Battalion to reach its position just as the Australian artillery barrage fell on Mont St. Quentin. Mactier was 28 years old and a sensible man; he could not have expected to live through such a desperate series of fights. His self-sacrifice was in the highest conduct of Australian arms.

The captured positions had now to be held. In an assault on September 1, the 6th Brigade passed over the line won by the 5th Brigade the day before, and its momentum carried it well over the crest of the mount. The fighting was bayonet work all the way and few prisoners were taken. The operation by the 2nd Division was completed on September 2, when the 7th Brigade came up in support behind the 6th. The 5th, having borne the brunt of the action, was relieved from further duty in the front line.

Congratulations reached the massively built Rosenthal in waves. Rawlinson's message read: "The capture of Mont St. Quentin by the 2nd Division is a feat of arms worthy of the highest praise. The natural strength of the position is immense and the tactical value of it, in reference to Peronne and the whole system of the Somme defences, cannot be overestimated. I am filled with admiration at the gallantry and surpassing daring of the 2nd Division in winning this important fortress and I congratulate them with all my heart." Monash sent General Rosenthal and his brigadiers "well-done" messages.

The Battle of Mont St. Quentin was the most brilliant victory of the AIF, and it was particularly sweet because it was wholly AIF planned and executed. Within Australian experience on the Western Front, it was the only important fight in which rapid and flexible manoeuvring played a decisive part. It was in many respects a soldiers' battle, in that once action was joined, it was not possible for the generals to exercise much influence over it. However, it was Monash's battle with "all his invariable care in planning, supplying and bridging", as C.E.W. Bean put it.

Soldiers' battle or generals' battle, the facts were that in the fighting at Mont St. Quentin and Peronne, the Australians attacked more than their number of Germans in strong positions and captured more of them than they could safely hold. Elements of three weakened Australian divisions dealt a staggering blow to five German divisions, including two elite ones.

The day after the Peronne fighting, the senior

Lewis-gunners of 54th Battalion keep watch in Peronne the day of its capture by Australian troops on September 2, 1918. In bitter street-by-street fightin

58th Battalion Lewis-gunners dislodged German mortar and machine-gun positions from every rubble heap.

German officer among the many in the officers' prison-cage asked permission to address about 100 other officers. Third Division HQ gave permission on the chance that the man might unwittingly reveal valuable information. Standing on a table, he told his comrades that they had fought a good fight, that their capture was not to their discredit, and that he would write them good reports, when he had the opportunity. On his own behalf and theirs, he wanted to express his admiration of the Australians' military prowess. Further, he freely acknowledged that his garrison had been outclassed, out-manoeuvred and outfought. The entire party then bowed to Monash's Intelligence officers who witnessed the scene. They knew that much of what the German said was nonsense. Many of the enemy had not "fought a good fight" and their capture had been discreditable.

Some Australian soldiers, fluent in German, were provided with enemy uniforms and told to grow a three-days' beard, so as to impersonate prisoners of war. Called "pigeons", these temporary spies were carefully instructed in what was expected of them and then taken under escort to a prisoners' cage near Peronne. Here a pigeon would spend a day or more in a compartment with specially selected genuine prisoners. When he was ready to leave he made a secret sign to the guard and an escort party would later arrive to take him to the Intelligence officers for "interrogation". The Australian pigeons were credited with obtaining much valuable information, such as details of the number of artillery pieces and machine-guns in the Hindenburg Line.

The 2nd Division had 84 officer casualties and 1,286 others in the Battle of Mont St. Quentin and its linked actions. The 3rd Division suffered 43 and 544; the 5th Division, 44 and 1,026. This was 20 per cent of the attacking force and showed that the victory, though decisive, had not been a walkover. German casualties were estimated at 3,500 and another 2,600 were taken prisoner. But the statistics were relatively unimportant in comparison with the strategic, tactical and psychological victory won by the Australians. Before the end of the first week of September, the Somme had passed into AIF history. The Germans were on the move and further battle was imminent.

Soon after the AIF's success at Mont St. Quentin and Peronne, a party of newspaper proprietors and editors from Australia visited the front. Haig agreed to talk to them and, unannounced, he spoke about the need for extending the death penalty to the AIF. He was convinced that the Australians, being subject to no death penalty and therefore, in his mind, afflicted with a high rate of desertion and absence without leave, was a central danger to his Army's discipline. The Field Marshal's visitors were astonished.

Haig had exaggerated the problem. The desertion rate, at less than 0.5 per cent, during the period May 1917 to June 1918, was lower than in other armies. Absence without leave was probably higher, but most of those Diggers who did go AWL voluntarily reported back to take their punishment. In fact, most men who deserted were shell-shocked out of their minds. General J.H.T. Hobbs, commander of the 1st Division, took a particular interest in cases of desertion. When seven men of the 60th Battalion were found guilty of this crime, Hobbs himself interviewed them and suspended the sentences. In one case a soldier had gone away to look after a French girl who had become seriously ill after having his baby.

Hobbs's Deputy Assistant Adjutant General, Lieutenant Colonel E.M. Ralph, instructed commanding officers not merely to look at the court records of men found guilty but to talk to the men themselves. Hobbs and Ralph believed that few men were deserters in the conventional military sense of deliberately trying to avoid action. Some left their units when out of the line because they were bored. Australians brought some of the stress they suffered upon themselves because they were never content merely to hold the line or capture and consolidate in an attack, as many other troops were. At all levels of rank, they went out of their

MUTINY ON THE WESTERN FRONT

Despite the heroism of many individual soldiers and the steady devotion to duty of most of them, a crisis developed within the AIF in 1918. Some Diggers bitterly complained that the Australian battalions were being asked to do more than their share. On July 8, the overtired men of the 59th Battalion, which had recently taken part in the Battle of Hamel, refused to leave their camp to return to the front. It was the first recorded mutiny in the AIF.

The men were eventually persuaded to go forward and they spent seven hard days in the front line near Peronne. But a mere two hours after being relieved and taken out, on September 14, the unit was ordered back to battle. This time the officers and men of three platoons refused to go and nobody could change their decision. They were too exhausted to fight and they wanted 5th Division Headquarters to know it. No action was taken over the incident.

On September 18, the illustrious 1st Battalion, under Lieutenant Colonel B.V. Stacey, came out of the fighting for the Hindenburg Outpost Line. Already depleted, the Battalion had lost a third of its strength, but the men were ordered to return immediately. Leaderless through loss of officers, 119 men refused to go back. Spokesmen said that they were not getting a fair go and that "other people should do their share of the work."

The 1st Battalion incident caused a dilemma. The defaulters should have been charged with mutiny, the punishment for which was death, even in the AIF, but such a sentence would have destroyed the AIF and the whole of Australia would have been in uproar. The 119 were charged not with mutiny but with desertion and, with one exception, found guilty. Officially without a unit, the convicted men followed the 1st Division around for weeks until the matter was finalised. After a period in France, the NCOs were sent to Dartmoor Prison in England, and they stayed there until Anzac Day, 1919, when they were pardoned by King George V and then returned to Australia.

Ten Australian deserters on the run from the French military police sent them this jolly photograph of themselves attached to a provocatively polite note which ended, "Trusting nous jamais regardez vous encore. Au revoir!" (We hope we will never see you again!)

For quite another reason a series of other mutinies took place during September and October. On Field Marshal Haig's insistence, the numerically weakest AIF battalions were to be disbanded and the men sent to fellow units. This had happened earlier to the 36th, 47th and 52nd Battalions, and those men, though distressed and resentful, had obeyed. Now the 19th, 21st, 25th, 29th, 37th, 42nd, 54th and 60th were to be disbanded — and they objected.

After discussion, the soldiers of the 37th agreed to attend the final parade and to obey all orders except the final one, the order to march to their new battalion. The unit was paraded on September 22 and on the order to dismiss, the officers and sergeants duly "fell out" to safeguard their rank. The men refused to march off and were told that they would be considered absent without leave from their new unit.

Treating the matter as an industrial dispute, the 37th elected leaders, maintained discipline and kept good order. Throughout the crisis the unit elected as their commanders men of good character and with a reputation for being able to lead in battle.

When the men of the 54th Battalion mutinied over disbandment, their mobile field kitchens were taken away and no rations were issued. Men from the other battalions of the brigade sent half their rations to the 54th. Senior officers who tried to force the soldiers to obey orders to report to other battalions only succeeded in further alienating them. After two tense days a compromise was reached: the 54th and 56th would amalgamate but each group would keep their own colour patches.

Spokesmen for the 25th Battalion notified their commanders that they wished to be given the most dangerous task in the next great battle — but with their identity unchanged. After the fighting, they said, there would be no 25th Battalion left to break up, or they would leave such a splendid record that nobody would dare to disband it.

"The 25th from the first to last has been built on esprit de corps," the men wrote to their CO, Lieutenant Colonel W.M. Davis. "We have been taught that the regiment is everything. You have often told us that we must sacrifice everything for its honour. We have always obeyed you and we always will — in everything but what you now ask. We cannot obey you in this for that reason. We would sacrifice everything for the battalion."

Like the other disbandment battalions, the 60th disobeyed its commander's order to join the 59th. The men's brigade commander, Brigadier General "Pompey" Elliott, met the crisis head on. He told them that disbandment was in the best interests of the AIF and when he gave the order to dismiss, to become part of the 59th, the men obeyed.

The refusal to disband was not treated as a mutiny by any British or Australian authority. The great majority of senior Australian officers were privately proud of the men's loyalty to their units and their colours. The disbandment crisis proved, if nothing else, that battalion esprit de corps was the greatest binding force in the AIF.

A fake tank, weighing nonetheless a quarter of a tonne, is deployed on high ground overlooking Le Verguier to confuse the enemy on the morning of September 18, 1918. Monash's ruse was a resounding success.

way to find fighting and seemed unaware of the penalty they paid in stress.

According to General Hobbs and Colonel Ralph, most men charged with desertion needed counselling by sympathetic officers who understood the strain under which they lived. When acting in command of the Australian Corps during Monash's absence in London, Hobbs investigated a number of cases of desertion and questioned the men. He found that some were veterans of outstanding reputation who had become convinced that after years of fighting they could not survive another battle. Others had sunk into a pit of hopelessness about ever again seeing their people in Australia. In most cases he recommended suspension of sentences to give the men a chance to make good. Monash approved of this step when he returned, though some excellent Australian leaders thought that such "softness" was storing up trouble for the future. They were wrong; it didn't.

C.E.W. Bean guided the Australian Prime Minister over the Amiens battlefields between September 12 and September 16. Despite all the sources of intelligence available to him, Hughes was astounded at the immense role being played by the Australians and Canadians. He told Bean he simply had no idea of the decisive nature of the AIF's involvement in the battles which had been raging since August 8. He arranged for successive parties of leading British newspaper owners and journalists to visit the Australian sector, with complete freedom to move as they pleased. Hughes wanted the publicity so that Australian influence in any peace settlement would be greater. Monash wanted it to inspire his Corps.

But there was a grim side to it all. While Hughes was in London, he visited AIF clubs where many soldiers told him, "There'll be no AIF if they don't rest us soon." Their forthright comments impressed him and their implications depressed him. He decided on three reforms: the original Anzacs were to get home leave to Australia; the Australian infantry must be withdrawn for rest no later than October 15; and during winter the Corps would be transferred to a milder climate. In putting these demands to Field Marshal Sir Henry Wilson, Chief of the Imperial General Staff, Hughes said, "The Australian divisions are being used

In close coordination with artillery fire, soldiers of the 45th Battalion snipe at retreating German infantry as the 4th Division closes on the outer defences of the Hindenburg Line on September 18, 1918.

as shock troops. If the final effort is to be made in 1919, as I am advised, it is only right to conserve them.''

Wilson said that ships were not available to take the Anzacs home on leave. Hughes countered by saying that he would procure them. Wilson advised him to see Haig about withdrawal of the Australians in autumn. Hughes retorted that he would not see Haig or anybody else. The decision was that of the Australian Government. The third point was left in abeyance, but Wilson knew that he had lost the argument with the fiery little Australian Prime Minister.

Hughes meant what he said. In mid-September, an order reached General Birdwood, as nominal administrative commander of the Australian Corps, that 60 officers and men who had left Australia in 1914 were to be embarked at once for two months' home leave. The majority would necessarily come from the 1st and 4th Divisions, the oldest ones. Monash, who was using these two divisions in an offensive against the Hindenburg Line, was shocked by Hughes's plans. He agreed to them only after much persuasion from Birdwood, but Hughes would have had his way in any case.

September 18 was an extraordinary day for the AIF. Monash was driving to capture Le Verguier and Hargicourt, two villages that the Germans had turned into Hindenburg Line fortresses north west of St. Quentin. To make up for his lack of men, Monash doubled the machine-gun resources of the two battle divisions; this gave him 256 Vickers machine-guns on a front of 6,400 metres. To compensate for his insufficiency in tanks, he asked for dummy ones. The AIF Engineer and Pioneer units vied with each other in rapid tank manufacture. They raided dumps and stores of paint, hessian and timber and produced awesome looking tanks. The most convincing were selected, and before dawn on September 18 four men dragged out each dummy to its selected position.

At Le Verguier, the 15th Battalion was to skirt to the north, the 13th to the south and the 16th was to assault the village itself. It was a classic isolate-and-capture operation, the sort of tactic in which the AIF had come to excel in 1918. The 13th set off behind a creeping barrage and successfully cleared several enemy outposts.

Two of them fell to Sergeant Gerald Sexton, firing a Lewis gun from the hip, a difficult operation because of the gun's weight.

As the advance continued, some of the fog and smoke cleared and visibility increased. Sexton's officer, Lieutenant R.L. Price, spotted a field gun and a mortar on a bank ahead. Sexton led his section in a dash, shot the crew of the gun and raced still further, under steady fire, to deal with the enemy around the mortar. Finally, he returned to the bank and fired into various dugout entrances. Suddenly, 30 Germans ran out and surrendered. Sexton had single-handedly captured the headquarters of the German 58th Infantry Regiment. Two hours later, as orders came to continue the advance, Sexton went into the open several times to silence machine-guns. It came as no surprise to his mates that he was awarded the VC. They already knew him as a dinkum Digger; he had won the Distinguished Conduct Medal the month before for his courage in battle.

In part because of Sexton's example, all objectives were seized by the 13th and the other two battalions had equal success. Le Verguier belonged to Monash after four hours of battle. And, to the north at Hargicourt the 1st and 3rd Brigades scored another important, if somewhat unspectacular, victory.

The 1st Division had attacked with a total strength of 2,854 infantry; the 4th with 3,048. This was only a sixth of their normal strength and one out of every five men who went into battle was lost. Again the Australians swept over the Germans within a morning. In taking Le Verguier and Hargicourt they had opened the way to the Hindenburg Line itself.

But the 1st and 4th Divisions had fought their last battle of the war. Monash considered that their fighting careers, which had commenced three-and-a-half years before at Gallipoli and in the Egyptian desert, respectively, had ended in "a blaze of glory". The divisions were not disbanded but many officers and NCOs were soon taken into other divisions. The men themselves were taken by bus and train to the coast south west of Amiens to rest and recuperate, after which the divisions would be reformed. One of the 1st Battalion's men wounded on September 18 was Sergeant N.H. Osmond. It was his sixth wound and he told his mates he hoped it was his last fight; he doubted that his luck could hold to a seventh non-lethal wound. He had been wounded twice at Gallipoli and three times previously on the Western Front. He never had to test his luck, though. Within a few weeks he was on his way home aboard a hospital ship.

Monash typically was anxious to get on with the job of forcing the Hindenburg Line. It was a tremendous task for his powers of organisation. He had five divisions, of which two were now American, besides the whole of the Corps support troops. His 58 battalions of infantry, although understrength, still amounted to 30,000 men. In addition there were 20,000 technical troops, including engineers, pioneers and signallers, and more than 1,000 guns of all calibres, 200 tanks, a brigade of cavalry, a battalion of armoured cars, and numerous air squadrons. The subsidiary services included observation balloons, supply trains, ammunition columns, auxiliary horse transport, ambulances, motor convoys and mechanical transport, together with railway, veterinary, sanitary and labour units.

With the Germans anticipating a British offensive, a surprise attack was impossible. To take his major objectives of Bellicourt and Bony Villages, Monash opened, on the night of September 26, a 60-hour bombardment with every gun under his command.

For two years, the Germans had been using mustard gas against the British, but similar British shells did not become available until September 1918. The shipment, of 50,000 rounds, was given to the Australian Corps. Monash ordered the first 12 hours of the bombardment to be with mustard-gas shells against enemy living quarters, occupied defences and all approaches to them. It was probably the only occasion in the war when the British used mustard-gas shells, and the Germans, who had used the gas in much larger

Collapsed from exhaustion and the cruel cold of a Somme winter, a transport mule is hand-fed by a compassionate Digger.

MAN AND HORSE: SHARING THE LOAD

Although armies were slowly becoming motorised during the Great War, they still depended heavily on horses and mules. The AIF used horses, some of them of Australian origin brought from Egypt, to draw ambulances, general-service wagons and field guns, while packhorses and mules regularly carried panniers of shells, boxes of small-arms ammunition, water and rations to forward lines or isolated units.

To save manpower, the AIF used mules at night to take water tins as close as possible to the front line. Ten mules controlled by two minders could carry as much water as 60 men. During the bitter 1916-1917 winter at Flers, wounded men were evacuated on improvised sleds drawn across the mud by one or two horses. In emergencies, ambulance horses were commandeered for direct military purposes. In November 1916 at Flers, the front-line units planning an attack needed 600 scaling ladders so troops could climb out of their deep, muddy trenches to go over the top. Orders were issued that ambulance horses were to be used to transport the heavy ladders across the sea of mud on sleds normally used for the wounded. The heavy labour wore out the horses, but most ladders were delivered in time for the attack.

Endlessly toiling along tracks, the thousands of packhorses and mules made them almost impassable. At places in the Ypres Salient during the 1917 offensive, horses pulling ammunition wagons sometimes became trapped in treacherous areas of mud and sank almost out of sight. The drivers struggled to keep the animals' heads up until help arrived.

The country-bred Australian drivers were regarded as the finest on the Front. In winter conditions, Australian drivers were dirty and their wagons battered, but their horses were groomed and in good condition. When strings of wagons were shelled, all soldiers in the vicinity dived for cover, but no shell-fire could separate an Australian wagon driver from his beloved horses. Horses at the halt trembled when they heard the whine of an incoming shell and instinctively buried their muzzles in their soldier-minders' chests.

Many animals were wounded, particularly by shell-fire, and among the busiest units were the Mobile Veterinary Sections. The 2nd Division's MVS was shelled in the back area in the summer of 1916 and reported that its horse patients suffered acute shell-shock. On August 21, enemy planes dropped seven bombs on the wagon lines of the 7th Field Artillery Battery in Becourt Wood, near Albert. Apart from the soldier casualties, 15 horses were killed and 29 wounded.

About 80,000 horses and mules in British service died on the Western Front. Australian fighting men, always sentimental about their horses, swore with anger when they came across animals gasping piteously for breath after a German gas attack. And when parted from their horses at the end of the war, tough Digger drivers often wept. The bonds they had forged with their four-legged mates were as strong as those they had made with their fellow soldiers.

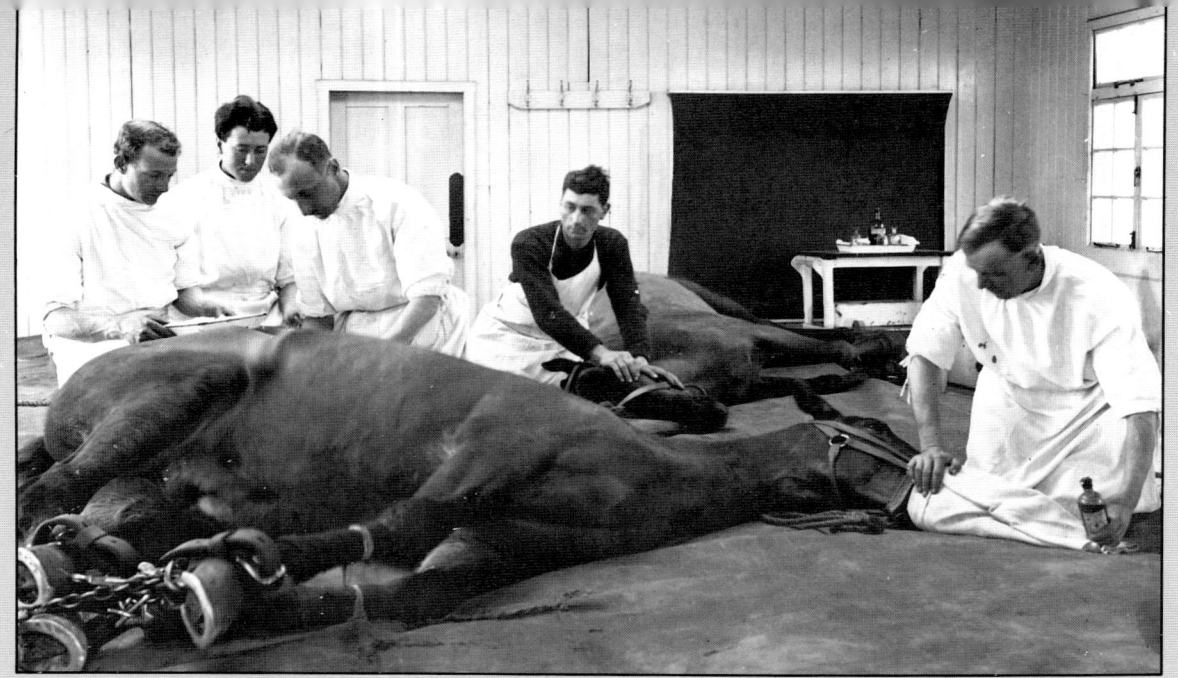

Surgeons at an AIF veterinary hospital in Calais work hard to save a wounded horse anaesthetised by chloroform. The Australian Light Horse Regiment saw little action in France; the highest horse casualties were among artillery teams.

A proud mule driver demonstrates with slouch hats the strength and size of his animal's ears.

Above: An officer pays a visit to the blacksmith's shop at an AIF Motor Transport Company base. Thick mud and debris played havoc with horses' feet and it was essential that they were well-shod. Left: Wearing veils as protection from summer flies, a line of well-groomed, fed and watered horses of the 14th Field Ambulance stand in a "bomb-shelter" trench behind the lines. Below: A gas-masked driver prepares his horses for a gas attack.

quantities, were horrified by their casualties.

The main weight of the high explosive bombardment fell on the German defences and especially on the barbed wire. Much of the wire in the Hindenburg Line was concealed, either in depressions in the ground or in specially dug moats. Such wire was difficult to locate and even more difficult to deal with. In the earlier years of the war, shrapnel shells, essentially killing projectiles, and high explosive shells, which smashed defences and gouged great holes in the ground, had failed to destroy wire. Monash's gunners were now equipped with the new British instantaneous 106 fuse. Shells so fused exploded on meeting the slightest obstacle, even a single strand of wire. The explosions uprooted wire entanglements and blew them aside, opening paths to the infantry.

The fighting lasted a full week and exhausted the 3rd and 5th Divisions. After 60 days of almost continuous battle their strength was so reduced that they were forced to leave the line to reorganise. The only Australian division remaining to Monash was the 2nd. Like the 1st and 4th Divisions, the 3rd and 5th had fought their final battles. Monash had once said that a hot bath and a week's rest restored a division's elasticity. But the AIF divisions needed much more than that.

The 2nd Division was left to fight the AIF's last battles in France, aimed at capturing the Beaurevoir Line and the fortified town of Montbrehain. The division went into action on a front of 5,500 metres, a very long length of battle front for a single undermanned division. Nevertheless, the whole of the Beaurevoir Line, a strong defence system, was taken before midday on October 3. The Australians captured 1,000 prisoners and many machine-guns.

Two days later, at 6.50 am, Major General Rosenthal, aided by tanks, launched his attack on Montbrehain itself. Before the fight, the men of B Company, 24th Battalion, sang: "A takes the right flank, D takes the left flank, But B'll be in Montbrehain before you." In fact, B Company had a particularly difficult advance. The platoon led by Lieutenant George Ingram was held up by a strong point, against which Ingram led a rush. The Germans resisted stubbornly, but Ingram's platoon killed 42 of them and captured nine machine-guns. Many more remained and while his men were mopping up, Ingram went on ahead, looking for other machine-gun nests. He found and shot a gunner who had been firing through a cellar ventilator, then burst into the back of the house and captured the garrison of 30. He was credited that day with having personally taken 62 prisoners.

Casualties in the 24th were so heavy that it borrowed two companies of the 27th for close support. Not until after 8 pm was the objective finally taken. Even then, the Germans, who had been ordered to hold Montbrehain at all costs, raided the Australian lines. For his actions that day, which effectively sealed the fate of Montbrehain, Ingram won the VC. It was the last Australian VC of the war in Europe and the Australians' last battle.

After a period of blessed rest and reinforcement, what was left of the reorganised 1st and 4th Divisions — 10,000 out of a paper strength of 40,000 — started back into the line in the north of France during the first week of November. But on November 11, the last day of the war, only a few AIF specialist troops were at or near the front. The end of the conflict came as an anti-climax and few men expressed any particular feelings about it. Private T.J. Cleary of the 17th Battalion wrote: "We had two victories today. We won the war and we defeated the 5th Company at soccer. The news of the Armistice was taken very coolly. Nobody seemed able to realise it."

Precisely 416,809 Australians, about 40 per cent of those eligible for service, enlisted in the AIF during the Great War. Of that number, 331,000 embarked for service abroad. The majority, about 295,000 served on the Western Front. One man in five, or a total of 63,163, died on active service. Another 156,128 were wounded. These terrible casualties amounted to 65 per cent of those who embarked with the AIF, and by far the majority of them, 179,537 to

A happy group of 1914 veterans are among the first entrained for Calais and the long trip home.

be exact, were suffered on the Western Front. Notably, only 4,084 Australians were taken prisoner during the entire war, 3,848 on the Western Front.

In the period March 27 to October 5, 1918 the Australian Army Corps of five divisions represented a little less than 10 per cent of the whole of the British forces on the Western Front, but its presence was far, far greater, even in the cold light of statistics. The Australians captured 23 per cent of the prisoners, 23½ per cent of the enemy guns and 21½ per cent of the ground wrested from the Germans.

Monash said that the AIF's success depended "first and foremost upon the military proficiency of the Australian private soldier and his glorious spirit of heroism." In his assessment: "The Australian Army was composed of the flower of the youth of the Continent. Mentally the Australian soldiers were well endowed. In him there was a curious blend of a capacity for independent judgment with a readiness to submit to self-effacement in a common cause.

"He had a personal dignity all his own. He had the political sense well developed and was always a keen critic of the way in which his battalion or battery was run and of the policies which guided his destinies from day to day. His adaptability saved him much hardship. He knew how to make himself comfortable. To light a fire and cook his food was a natural instinct. A sheet of corrugated iron, a batten or two and a few strands of wire were enough to enable him to fabricate a home in which he would live at ease. Psychologically, he was easy to lead but difficult to drive. His imagination was readily fired. War to him was a game and he played with enthusiasm. His bravery was founded upon his sense of duty to his unit, comradeship to his fellows, emulation to uphold his traditions, and a combative spirit to avenge his hardships and sufferings upon the enemy."

War might have been a game for a short time, but Australian soldiers soon lost all idea that it was some kind of sport. On the Western Front, it was a deadly dangerous way of life from which the only honourable escape seemed to be a disabling wound or illness, or death itself. To live through the war and become a "returned man" was the great but improbable ambition.

The Digger drew his motivation from his profound sense of mateship and his pride in his origins as an Australian. "From the beginning they said we were different," said one veteran. "We had to prove that we were."

In August 1919, devoted French children tend the graves of Australian soldiers at Villers-Bretonneux. A deep bond of affection and respect for the brave sons of Australia who fought and died in France is expressed in a placard in every Villers-Bretonneux classroom: 'N'oublions jamais l' Australie'' (Never forget Australia).

BIBLIOGRAPHY

Adam-Smith, Patsy. *The Anzacs*. Melbourne: Nelson, 1978
Allan, P.V. *The Thirty-Ninth*. Sydney: Green & Sons, 1934
Barrie, Alexander. *War Underground*. London: Frederick Muller, 1962
Bean, C.E.W. *Official History of Australia in the War of 1914-1918, Vols. IV, V and VI*. Sydney: Angus & Robertson, 1921-1943.
Belford, W.C. *Legs Eleven (11th Battalion)*. Perth: Imperial Printing Co., 1940
Bickel, L. *In Search of Frank Hurley*. Melbourne: Macmillan, 1980
Bridger, T.D. *With the 27th Battery in France*. Sydney: 1919
Cariselle, P.J. and James W. Ryan. *Who Killed the Red Baron?* New York: 1969
Charlton, Peter. *Pozieres 1916 — Australians on the Somme*. London: Leo Cooper and Secker & Warburg, 1986
Chataway, T.P. *History of the 15th Battalion*. Melbourne: William Brooks & Co., 1948
Collett, H.B. *The 28th, a Record of War Service with the AIF*. Perth: Library, Museum & Art Gallery, 1922
Cutlack, F.M. *The Australians: Their Final Campaigns, 1918*. London: Sampson Low, 1920
——. *The Official History of Australia in the War of 1914-1918, Vol. VIII, The Australian Flying Corps*. Sydney: 1923
——. *War Letters of General Monash*. Sydney: Angus & Robertson, 1934
Cuttries, G.P. *"Over the Top" With the Third Australian Division*. Sydney: Charles H. Kelly, 1920
Devine, W. *The Story of a Battalion (48th)*. Melbourne: 1919
Ellis, A.D. *The Story of the Fifth Australian Division*. London: Hodder & Stoughton, 1920
Fairey, Eric. *The 38th Battalion AIF*. Bendigo: 38th Battalion History Committee, 1920
Gammage, Bill. *The Broken Years*. Canberra: National University Press, 1974
Gilbert, A. *World War I in Photographs*. London: Macdonald Orbis, 1987
Giles, J. *The Ypres Salient*. London: Leo Cooper, 1970
Gorman, Captain E. *With the Twenty-Second*. Melbourne: H.H. Champion, 1919
Green, F.C. *The Fortieth. A Record of the 40th Battalion*. Hobart: Government Printer, 1922
Harvery, W.J. *The Red and White Diamond (24th Battalion)*. Melbourne: Alexander McCubbin, 1920
Harvey, K.N. *From Anzac to the Hindenburg Line (9th Battalion)*. Brisbane: 1941
Knyvett, Captain R. Hugh. *"Over There" With the Australians*. New York: Charles Scribner's Sons, 1918
Laffin, J. *Digger: Legend of the Australian Soldier*. Melbourne: Macmillan, 1986
Lock, C.B.L. *The Fighting 10th Battalion*. Adelaide: Webb, 1936
Longmore, C. *Eggs-a-Cook! (44th Battalion)*. Perth: 1921
——. *The Old Sixteenth*. Perth: 1929
Maxwell, Joe. *Hell's Bells and Mademoiselles*. Sydney: Angus & Robertson, 1932
McKenzie, K.W. *The Story of the Seventeenth Battalion*. Sydney: Shipping Newspapers Ltd., 1946
McKernan, Michael. *Padre: Australian Chaplains in Gallipoli and France*. London: Allen and Unwin, 1986
——. *The Australian People and the Great War*. Sydney: Collins, 1984
Mitchell, G.D. *Backs to the Wall*. Sydney: Angus & Robertson, 1937
Monash, Lieutenant General Sir John. *The Australian Victories in France in 1918*. London: Hutchinson, 1924
Odgers, G. *The Royal Australian Air Force: An Illustrated History*. Brookvale: Child and Henry, 1984
Paterson, A.T. et al. *The Thirty-Ninth*. Melbourne: 1934
Rule, E.J. *Jacka's Mob*. Sydney: Angus & Robertson, 1933
Robson, L.L. *The First AIF. A Study of its Recruitment 1914-1918*. Melbourne: Melbourne University Press, 1970
Sloan, H. *The Purple and Gold (30th Battalion)*. Sydney: 1938
Smithers, A.J. *Sir John Monash*. London: Leo Cooper, 1973
Stacy, B.V. et al. *The History of the 1st Battalion AIF*. Sydney: Angus & Robertson, 1931
Taylor, A.J.P. *The First World War. An Illustrated History*. Middlesex: Penguin, 1985
Taylor, F.W. and T.A. Cusack. *Nulli Secundus. A History of the Second Battalion AIF*. Sydney: New Century Press. 1942
Titler, Dale M. *The Day the Red Baron Died*. New York: 1970
White, T.A. *The Fighting Thirteenth*. Sydney: 1924
Wigmore, Lionel. *They Dared Mightily*. Canberra: Australian War Memorial, 1963.
Wren, E. *Randwick to Hargicourt (3rd Battalion)*. Sydney: Angus & Robertson, 1935

PICTURE ESSAY QUOTES

CHARITY BEGINS AT HOME: "Men must fight and women must knit socks." *Charivari*, Ascham school magazine.
ON MENIN ROAD: "A land of horror and dread whence few return." Hugh Quigley, *Passchendaele and the Somme*.
HEROES WITHOUT GUNS: "Don't forget me cobber." Lieutenant Simon Fraser, 58th Battalion, describing the work of stretcher-bearers.
DIGGER: "They put laughter into everything." Phillip Harris, *Aussie* magazine.

Zealand, 26, 40, 41, 45, 58; British 1st Cavalry, 60; British 8th, 69; 4th German Guard, 73 Moroccan, 76, 115; Wurttemberg, 116; 2nd Prussian Guards, 144; 43rd Reserve, 105; British 47th, 130
Duke, Captain C.R. 129
Dyson, Will, 8, 26, 54, 90, 114, 142

E
Elles, Brigadier General Hugh, 101
Elliott, Brigadier General H.E. "Pompey", 37, 40, 65; and 15th Bde at Villers-Bretonneux 68-73
Etineham, *map* 118-119, 127
Evans, Captain D.G., 31
Evans, Private "Snowy", 74

F
Fairweather, Captain F.E., 55
Feuilleres, 144, *map* 145
Flanders, 8, 9, *map* 11, 12, 15, 17, 88, 90, 115
Flanders 1 Line, *map* 28, 36, 37, 127
Flaque, La, *map* 118-119, 130
Flers, 157
Florina Trench, 147, 149
Foch, Marshal, 77, 114, 115
Franvillers, *map* 63, 92
Fraser, Lieutenant Simon, 108
Fromelles, *map* 11
Fynch, Sergeant R.A., 73

G
Gaby, Lieutenant Alfred, VC 124, 127
Gellibrand, Brigadier General John, 90, 96, 143, 147
George V, *10*, 129
Gheluvelt Ridge, 12
Glasgow, Brigadier General T.W., 69-73, 77, 96
Glencorse Wood, *map* 28, 30, 31
Glisy, *map* 63, 71, 148
Gottlieb Trench, 145, *map* 145
Gough, General Sir Hubert, 12, 15, 27, 96
Gravenstafel Spur, *map* 28, 40
Graves Registration Unit, 82
Grogan, Brigadier General VC, 77

H
Haig, General Sir Douglas, 9-13, 15, 17, 26, 27; at Passchendaele, 41, 45; 54, 55, 96; and the battle for Hamel, 103, 105; 115, 127, 129; 142, 146; and the death penalty, 152; 153, 155
Hamel, 60 *map* 63, 91, 101-105, 114, 115, *map* 118, 135, 145, *map* 145
Hamel, Battle of, 148, 153
Hammond, Captain M.G., 100
Hangard Wood, *map* 63, 68, 71
Hannebeek Swamp, *map* 28, 30
Happy Valley, *map* 118-119, 130
Harbonnieres, *map* 11, 63, *map* 118-119, 124, 125
Hargicourt, *map* 145, 155, 156
Harrington, Lieutenant W.G., 13
Harrison, Lieutenant P.W., 15
Hartt, Cecil, 123
Hayes, Company Quarter Master Sergeant J.C., 125, 126
Hazebrouk, *map* 11, 17, *map* 55, 91
Hebuterne, *map* 11, *map* 56, 58, *59*
Hell Fire Corner, *map* 28, 48, *49*
Henderson, Captain R.J., 91
Heneker, Major General W.C., 69, 71, 72
Herleville Wood, *map* 118-119, 131
Hill 60, *map* 28, 48
Himes, Private J., *117*
Hindenburg Line, 142, 143, *map* 145, 147, 152, 153, 155, 156, 160
Hobbs, Major General J.T.T., 152-154
Holman, Premier (NSW) W.A. 10
Holmes, Major General W., 10, 12
Hughes, Prime Minister W.M., *33*, and 33, 54, 154, 155
Hurley, Frank, 6-7, 38-39

I
Ingram, Lieutenant George, VC, 160
Iron Cross Redoubt, *map* 28, 30
Irvine, Lieutenant A.W., 92

J
Jacka, Captain Albert, VC, 37, 130
Jeffries, Captain Clarence, VC, 45
Jenkins, Lieutenant F.J., 147, 149

K
Keiburg Spur, 45
Kennedy, Sergeant H.H., 68
Kilminster, Private A.H., 84
King, Captain R., 97

L
Lavarack, Lieutenant Colonel J.D., 58
Lean, Corporal J., 91
Leane, Lieutenant Colonel Ray, 76
Liaison Force, 126
Lice, 126
Lihons, *map* 118, 127, 143, *map* 145
Lille, *map* 11, 13
Line, Blue, 30, *map* 31; Red, 30
Little, Captain R.A., 97
Lloyd George, Prime Minister David, 9, 55
Longstaff, William, 52, 53
Lovett, Captain N.B., 68
Lowdon, Sergeant K., 82
Lowerson, Sergeant David, VC, 147
Ludendorff, Field Marshal Erich Von, 55, 60, 76, 79, 92, 114, 115, 126, 144
Lys River, *map* 11, 55, *map* 56, 77
Lys River Valley, 100, 115

M
Mackay, Brigadier General Iven, 125
Mactier, Private Robert, VC, 147, 148
Madame Wood, *map* 118-119, 130
Mangin, General Charles, 114, 115
Mann, Lieutenant A.W., 91
Manton, Major R.G., 17
Marwitz, General Von der, 105
McCarthy, Lieutenant Lawrence, VC, 131
McCloughry, Captain, E.J.K., 97, *99*
McDougall, Sergeant Stan, VC, 60
McGee, Sergeant Lewis, VC, 41
McInerney, Lieutenant J.M., 100
McNamara, Lieutenant F.H., 97
Menin, *map* 11, *map* 56
Menin Gate, *map* 28, 48, *52-53*
Menin Road, *map* 28, 29, *46-53*, 48
Menin Road, Battle of, 27, 29, *31*, 32, *38-39*, 41, *51*
Merris, 100, 101, 114
Messines, 8-10, *map* 11, 12, 26, *map* 56, 69, 80, 148
Mitchell, Lieutenant H.F., 76
Molenaarelshoek, *map* 28; 40
Monash, Major General Sir John, 10, 37, 55, 58, 90, 91; placed in command of Australian Corps, 96; 100; and battle for Hamel, 101-105; 114, 116, 124, 127, 128; knighted, 129; at Mont St. Quentin, 142-147; *148*; 149, 152, 154, 160, 162
Montbrehain, *map* 145, 160
Montgomery, Major General Archibald, 146
Mont St. Quentin, *map* 11, *map* 56, 56, 142-149; *map* 145, 152
Monument Wood, *map* 63, 73, 76, *map* 118-119

Moore, Captain F.L., 32
Morcourt, *map* 118-119, 120
Morlancourt, *map* 63, 92, 94, 100, 101, 116
Morshead, Lieutenant Colonel L.J., 146
Mouquet Farm, 58, 80, *90*

N
Nieuport, *map* 11, 12
No-Man's-Land, 9, *14,* 55, 76, 90, 135
Nonne Boschen, *map* 28, 30

O
Ommiecourt, 144, *map* 145
Operation George 1, 63
Operation, Michael, 57, 63
Osmond, Sergeant N.H., 156

P
Passchendaele, *map* 11, 12, 13, 26, *map* 28, 45, 100
Peck, Lieutenant Colonel J.H., 37
Peeler, Lance Corporal Walter, VC, 41, 43
Peronne, *map* 11, *map* 56, 131, 142, 144, *map* 145, 147, 149, 150, 152
Petain, Marshal Henri, 8,9, *10,* 55
Pilckem, *map* 11, *map* 28
Pilckem Ridge, Battle of, 11, 13, *14*
Ploegsteert Wood, *map* 11
Plumer, General Sir Herbert, 9, 10, 12; at Passchendaele, 26-29 54, 148
Polygon Wood, *map* 28, 32, 36, 117
Polygon Wood, Battle of *36, 41*
Popkin, Sergeant Cedric, 74
Pozieres, *map* 11, *map* 56, 58, 76, 80
Proyart, *map* 11, *map* 118-119, 127

R
Ralph, Lieutenant Colonel E.M., 152, 154
Rawlinson, General Sir Henry, 9, 12, 77, 115, 127; and battle for Mont St. Quentin, 144-146; 148
Rayner, Sergeant G.P., 15
RE8 (aircraft), 97, *97, 99*
Regiments, 212th German, 41; 62nd German, 92; 131st American, 127; Kaiserin Augusta, 144, 146; Kaiser Alexander, 144, 146; German 58th Infantry, 156; Australian Light Horse, 158
Rheims, *map* 11, *map* 56, 114
Richthofen, Baron von, 68, 74, *74-75*
Roberts, Corporal E.E.V., 13
Roberts, Private F.W., 102
Rosenthal, Brigadier General Charles, 60, 96, 144, 147, 148, 160
Rosieres, *map* 118-119, 130
Ruthven, Sergeant William, VC, 94

S
Sadlier, Lieutenant Clifford, VC, 73, 76
Sailly Laurette, *map* 63, 100, *map* 118-119
Sinclair-Maclagan, Major General E.W., 12, 13, 58, 102
Smith, Assistant Provost Marshal Major W., 17
Smithers, A.J., 148
Soissons, *map* 56, 115
Somme River, *map* 11, 15, *map* 63, 69, 71, 74, 101, 115, *map* 118-119, 144, *map* 145
Sopwith Camel, 74, 97, *98*
Squadrons, 209 (RAF), 74; No. 1 (AFC), 97; No. 2 (AFC), 97; No. 3 (AFC), 55, 97, *97,* 102, 116; No. 4 (AFC), 97, *99*
St. Pol, *map* 56; 57
Staples, Lieutenant H.E., 68
Statton, Sergeant Percy, VC, 128, 129
Stokes, Sergeant Charlie, 73
Stretcher Bearer, *106-113,* 108

T
Tanks, British Mk. IV, 69; German A7V, 69; Whippet, 69; British Mk V, 101, 104, *104,* 124
Tokio Ridge, *map* 28, 36
Towner, Lieutenant Edgar, VC, 147
Tucker, Lieutenant F.G., 13

U
Units, Engineer, 155; Pioneer, 155; Mobile Veterinary Sections (MVS), 157; 14th Field Ambulance, *159*

V
Vaire, *map* 63, 103
Varley, Lieutenant A.S., 13, 15
Veldhoek Ridge, 27, *map* 28
Verguier, Le, *map* 145, 154, 155, 156
Versailles, 104
Ville-sur-Ancre, *map* 63, 94, *94,* 96, 101, 103
Villers-Bretonneux, *map* 11, *map* 56, *map* 60, 68, 69, 71, *72,* 76, 77, *77-78,* 80, 84, 101, 103, 115, 116, *map* 118-119, 127, 128, 139, 163
Volunteer Detachment Nurses, *20*

W
Wackett, Captain, L.J., 102
Walker, General N.B., 96
Walker, Major General H.B., 26
Wanliss, Captain Harold, 37
Warneton Line, 10
Weathers, Corporal Lawrence, VC, 147
Western Front, *map* 11, 15, 27, 55, 91, 120, 162
Westhoek Ridge, *map* 28, 30, 48, 99
White, Major General Cyril Brudenell, 17, 27, 28, 32, 36, 41, 54, 96, 148
Wilder-Neligan, Lieutenant Colonel, 31, 100
Wilhelm Line, *map* 28, 31
Wilson, Field Marshal Sir Henry, 127, 154, 155
Wiltshire, Lieutenant J.A., 96
Wisdom, Brigadier General E.A., 100, 127

Y
Young, Captain E.M., 73
Ypres, 10, *map* 11, 12, 13, 16, 27, 29, *31, 44,* 69
Ypres, Second Battle of, 41
Ypres, Third Battle of, 3, 12, 15, 45, 148
Yser River, 9, *map* 11

Z
Zeebrugge, 12
Zonnebeke. *3, map* 28, *36,* 48